W9-BZT-147

H·E·L·P

WITH

PHRASAL VERBS

RICHARD ACKLAM

HEINEMANN

Heinemann International
A division of Heinemann Publishers (Oxford) Ltd,
Halley Court, Jordan Hill, Oxford, OX2 8EJ

OXFORD   LONDON   EDINBURGH
MADRID   PARIS   ATHENS   BOLOGNA
MELBOURNE   SYDNEY   AUCKLAND   SINGAPORE   TOKYO
IBADAN   NAIROBI   GABORONE
HARARE   PORTSMOUTH (NH)

ISBN 0 435 281143
Help with Phrasal Verbs is accompanied by a cassette
ISBN 0 435 281151
© Richard Acklam 1992
First published 1992

All rights reserved; no part of this publication may be
reproduced, stored in a retrieval system, or transmitted in any
form or by any means, electronic, mechanical, photocopying,
recording, or otherwise, without the prior written permission
of the Publishers.

Text acknowledgements
Our thanks are due to the following for their kind permission
to reproduce a text: *BT*, Business Catalogue Advertisement,
1989 (p 18); *Collins* COBUILD Dictionary of Phrasal Verbs
1989, own up, go on 9 (p 69), get up to, show up (p 70), talk
into, pop in (p 71), tell off (p 72); *Health Education Authority*,
A Smoker's Guide to Giving Up, 'How They Gave Up' (p 55);
The Independent, Summary column 14.9.90 (p 42); *Longman*
Dictionary of Phrasal Verbs 1983, come into (p 69) end up 1
(p 71), R Courtney; *Mary Glasgow Publications*, Practical
English Teaching, 'Phrasal verbs – domino style', José-Luis
Ibáñez and Pablo Ferŕin Dengan (pp 72, 73); by permission of
Oxford University Press, Oxford Dictionary of Current
Idiomatic English (vol. 1, Phrasal Verbs, 1975), sort out (p 70)
branch out (p 71).

Photograph and artwork acknowledgements
We would like to thank the following for permission to
reproduce photographs and artwork: *AA Picture Library*,
terrace houses (p 49); *Aquarius/© Touchstone, Disney*, Dick
Tracy, Columbo, Magnum, MCA (p 63); *Paul Freestone*,
children in school, schoolboy (p 50); *Health Education
Authority*, Giving up smoking (p 54); *ITN's Channel 4 News/
Jon Snow*, News presenter (p 39); *Archie Miles*, executive
woman, executive man (p 5), woman, man (p 55); *PA*,
aggressive football fans (p 9); *PA/Topham*, Football Pools
winners (p 29); reproduced by permission of *Punch*, I feel old
age creeping up on me – it's nearly four-thirty ... (p 57), I know
the pet shop said he'd been well looked after but this is
ridiculous. (p 53), Is it cheaper to fill up with litres or gallons?
(p 34), They've always got on wonderfully together. (p 24),
Your wife wants to know if you'll agree to have him put down.
(p 41), Well, really! You'd think by now he'd have picked up
English. (p 4); *Alan Spence*, detached house (p 49).

Illustrations by Sue Heap, Jane Applebee, Harriet Dell
Designed by Greg Sweetnam, Gina Smart

Phototypeset by Tradespools Ltd, Frome, Somerset
Printed and bound in Great Britain by The Bath Press, Avon
92 93 94 95 96 10 9 8 7 6 5 4 3 2 1

Contents

NB. All units marked with an * contain listening material that you
can find on the *Help with Phrasal Verbs* cassette.

Introduction for Teachers

The aim of this book

Many students at an intermediate level are aware that phrasal verbs represent an important area which they need to confront. Often students are able to avoid using them by replacing them with Latinate 'equivalents', for example, *tolerate* in place of *put up with*. However, this can result in students sounding, at best, unnatural, and, at worst, pompous. Nevertheless they may succeed in communicating their basic meaning. More seriously, both general and business English students will find that, on a receptive level, native-speaker speech and writing is littered with phrasal verbs in both informal and more formal contexts. Phrasal verbs are also regularly tested in both Cambridge First Certificate and Proficiency examinations.

Help with Phrasal Verbs aims to enable students to both understand and use approximately 130 common phrasal verbs with confidence and accuracy.

Structure and organisation

Help with Phrasal Verbs consists of 15 units, each dealing with between 8 and 10 different phrasal verbs, plus 3 revision units and a test. The phrasal (or multi-word) verbs dealt with are all more or less idiomatic ie the meaning cannot be deduced from a knowledge of the constituent elements.

Each unit provides around one and a half hours work (plus a Writing Task, which can be used as homework), depending on the level of your students and how long you spend on each section.

The units are organised as integrated and complete lessons in their own right. There are a range of activities employing each of the skills of listening or reading, speaking and writing and differing degrees of focus on accuracy and fluency depending on the particular stage of the unit.

The texts for each unit alternate between being spoken and written as it is important for students to be exposed to phrasal verbs in both contexts. All the spoken texts are on the accompanying cassette. The tapescripts for these can all be found at the back of the book, if you wish to refer students to them at any stage.

In most units many of the phrasal verbs are linked to a particular topic, for example, telephoning. However, the units also contain other phrasal verbs in order to avoid missing out certain important phrasal verbs which do not tie in to some clearly identifiable theme.

Every sixth unit is a Revision Unit which includes most of the phrasal verbs covered in the previous five units, helping to consolidate them as part of the students' productive repertoire through a variety of different exercise types.

Before Unit 1 there is a section on the grammar of phrasal verbs. This will not necessarily be appropriate for all students but is provided so that students who are interested in this kind of analysis can see for themselves how different phrasal verbs operate. The grammar type of each phrasal verb is given both within each unit and at the end of the book in the Reference Section.

Methodology

Each unit has a basically similar structure:

- ARTWORK AND INTRODUCTORY DISCUSSION QUESTION (to get students thinking around the main topic of the unit)

  Put students in pairs or groups to discuss these opening questions and then get feedback from the class.

  NB You may wish at this point to pre-teach some of the more difficult vocabulary (not the phrasal verbs) that comes up in the text.

- TASK 1: GIST QUESTIONS (to give students a general task to do while they listen/read for the first time)

  Make sure that students know they are not expected to understand all the details of the text at this stage. For the reading texts encourage students to read quickly, just to answer the gist question, not worrying about particular vocabulary or sections that they don't understand.

  Let students discuss the questions before answering.

- TASK 2: SPECIFIC INFORMATION QUESTIONS (to help students to understand the text in more detail)

  At this stage students should try to understand the text in more detail. After reading or listening to the text for the second time let students discuss amongst themselves again and try to refer back to the text to justify their answers. If there are disagreements between students either play the tape again at the appropriate section or ask them to quote the part of the written text that justifies their answer. If students still cannot agree on the correct answer, explain why one particular answer is the right one.

- FOCUS ON PHRASAL VERBS (to help students pick out and understand the phrasal verbs in the text from the surrounding context)

At this point, ask the students, if they don't already know, to try to work out the meaning of the phrasal verbs from the surrounding context. Give students sufficient time to discuss and decide on a possible meaning of the phrasal verb in question.

- CONTROLLED PRACTICE (exercises to help reinforce the meaning of the phrasal verbs and to make students think about the grammar of the phrasal verbs)

It is probably better if students first attempt the controlled practice on their own so that they can see where their own difficulties lie. These exercises should reveal any remaining misunderstandings of meaning and any problems of form.

NB These may throw up other problems of grammar, for example, tenses. The extent to which you go into these will depend on the time available and the particular objectives of your class.

- FREE PRACTICE (an opportunity for students to speak, using the phrasal verbs in a less controlled context)

It is very important that students have the opportunity to put the phrasal verbs into their productive vocabulary. This section aims to do that. Students should not be interrupted during the tasks but you may like to go over any problems that have arisen after the task has been completed. Make it clear to the students that it is more important that they communicate their message than that they attempt to make no errors when speaking.

- WRITING TASK (an opportunity for students to confirm they have understood both when and how the new phrasal verbs can be used)

This task helps students consolidate their knowledge of the phrasal verbs of the particular unit and previous units. They can practise using them in new contexts and check that they have understood the grammatical limits on their use. It is important that students get written feedback from the teacher on the success with which they have included the various phrasal verbs. The writing task can be set as homework.

Revision and recycling

After every five units there is a special Revision Unit. Phrasal verbs recur within individual units as well, thus encouraging students as they realise that they are becoming familiar with key phrasal verbs. These phrasal verbs are printed in **bold**, while the new target phrasal verbs are printed in _italics_. If you are not working through the book systematically you may wish to pre-teach the phrasal verbs in **bold**, so that students are not distracted by them as they focus on the target phrasal verbs of the unit.

There is also a Special Test Section after Revision Unit 3 which tests students' knowledge of phrasal verbs in the same form as is sometimes found in the Cambridge First Certificate examination. All the phrasal verbs in this test have been taught earlier in the book.

Introduction for Students

What is a phrasal verb?

A phrasal verb is basically a main verb + a preposition or adverb, for example, *pick up, put down*. Unfortunately there are a number of phrasal verbs where the meaning is not so clear, for example,

He would like to **give up** *smoking.*

Here the phrasal verb is *give up*, but the meaning is not obvious. It is not possible to understand what it means just by understanding the words *give* and *up*. In this context *give up* means *stop* and there are a lot of phrasal verbs like this, where the phrasal verb has a special meaning.

How important are phrasal verbs?

- In speaking you can often avoid verbs by saying, for example, *stop* instead of *give up*. Unfortunately, it is not always so simple and if you don't use the phrasal verb you may sound unnatural, particularly in ordinary, everyday conversation. For example, it would sound very strange to an English-speaker if you said:

  He extinguished the cigarette.
    and not
  He **put** *the cigarette* **out**.

- In reading and listening you cannot avoid phrasal verbs, they are everywhere. Consequently, it is very important that you understand at least the most common.

- If you take the Cambridge First Certificate or Proficiency examinations you will be tested on your knowledge of phrasal verbs.

The aim of this book

Help with Phrasal Verbs helps you to both understand and use approximately 130 common phrasal verbs with confidence and accuracy.

Structure and organisation

Help with Phrasal Verbs consists of 15 units, 3 revision units and a test. There are between 8 and 10 different phrasal verbs in each unit.

Before Unit 1 there is a section on the **grammar** of phrasal verbs. This explains how to use individual phrasal verbs correctly, for example, if it is possible to separate the verb from the particle like this:

I would like to **give up** smoking.
I would like to **give** smoking **up**.
I would like to **give** it **up**.

This is not possible with all phrasal verbs.

The texts for each unit are alternately spoken and written. This means you will have practice in seeing and hearing the phrasal verbs in a variety of contexts you could meet in real life. All the spoken texts are on the accompanying cassette. The tapescripts for these are at the back of the book, if you want to refer to them.

Every sixth unit is a Revision Unit. In this unit most of the phrasal verbs included in the previous five units are revised through a variety of different exercise types. There is also a Special Test Section which tests your knowledge of a number of different phrasal verbs. The form of this test is the same as is sometimes used in the Cambridge First Certificate examination. All the phrasal verbs in this test have been taught earlier in the book. If you want to check the meaning or the grammar of a phrasal verb, you can look it up in the Reference Section which has information about all the phrasal verbs included in the book. All the answers to the exercises are in the Key at the end of the book.

Methodology

Each unit has a basically similar structure:

- ARTWORK AND INTRODUCTORY DISCUSSION QUESTION (to help you start thinking about the main topic of the unit)

- TASK 1: GIST QUESTIONS (to give you a general task to do while you listen/read for the first time)

  You are not expected to understand all the details of the text at this stage. For the reading texts read quickly, just to answer the gist questions. Unknown, new vocabulary should not stop you understanding the general idea. You can look at the meaning of these words later.

- TASK 2: SPECIFIC INFORMATION QUESTIONS (to help you understand the text more intensively)

- FOCUS ON PHRASAL VERBS (to help you understand the phrasal verbs in the text)

  Phrasal verbs printed in **bold** in the text are ones that have appeared before in earlier units, while the new target phrasal verbs are printed in *italics*.

- CONTROLLED PRACTICE (exercises to check you understand the meaning of the phrasal verbs and to help you think about the grammar of the phrasal verbs)

- FREE PRACTICE (an opportunity for you to speak, using the phrasal verbs more fluently)

  This section presents tasks which involve pairs or groups of students. If you are working alone you can record yourself doing the task on cassette. So, in Unit 1, for example, you will be talking about your experience of learning a new language. Try to speak without stopping about the particular subject, using the phrasal verbs from that unit and other units as appropriate. When you have finished, listen to the recording and then do it again, trying to improve on your first attempt. This will give you important practice in using the phrasal verbs in a more fluent way than in the **Controlled Practice** section.

- WRITING TASK (an opportunity for you to confirm you have understood both when and how the new phrasal verbs can be used)

The Grammar of Phrasal Verbs

A phrasal verb is essentially a verb and one or two additional particles, for example, *look for*, *put up with*.

There are four basic types of phrasal verbs. These are as follows:

Type 1 = verb + adverb (no object)

The verb and adverb cannot be separated in phrasal verbs of this category.

> Example: *break down* = stop working
> *The car **broke down** and we had to walk.*

With this meaning you cannot say *break* something *down* or *break down* something.

There is no passive form with Type 1 phrasal verbs.

Pronunciation: the adverb, and not the verb, is usually stressed with Type 1 phrasal verbs.

> Example: *The car **broke down** and we had to walk.*

Type 2 = verb + adverb + object/
verb + object + adverb

The verb and adverb can be separated.
- If the object is a noun, the adverb can come before or after the noun.
- If the object is a pronoun, for example, *it*, the adverb must come after the object.

> Example: *put off* = to postpone
> *We must **put off** the meeting for another week.*
> *We must **put** the meeting **off** for another week.*
> *We must **put** it **off** for another week.*
>
> > But not
>
> ~~We must **put off** it for another week.~~

Pronunciation: the adverb, and not the verb, is usually stressed with Type 2 phrasal verbs.

> Example: *We must **put** it **off** for another week.*

Type 3 = verb + preposition + object

The preposition cannot be separated from the verb.

> Example: *take after* = be similar to older relative
> *He **takes after** his mother.*
> *He **takes after** her.*
>
> > But not
>
> ~~He **takes** his mother **after**.~~
> ~~He **takes** her **after**.~~

Type 4 = verb + adverb + preposition + object

Phrasal verbs in this category have 2 particles. They cannot be separated from the verb.

    Example: *put up with* = tolerate
           *I can't **put up with** his behaviour any more.*
           *I can't **put up with** it any more.*

Pronunciation: the stress usually falls on the first particle.
    Example: *I can't **put <u>up</u> with** it any more.*

Practice

In each unit you will find the grammar type of the key phrasal verbs is given. Also in the Reference Section at the back of this book there is information about all the phrasal verbs we are going to look at, including which type each one is. To see if you can use the information about the grammar of phrasal verbs here are some sentences including phrasal verbs. We have given you the type of each phrasal verb. You must decide if the sentence is grammatically correct or not. If the sentence is not correct, correct it.

Example:
look at (*type 3*)   He looked them at for a long time.
                   NOT CORRECT
                   *He **looked at them** for a long time.*

a) get up (*type 1*)   He got up and walked across the room. ✓

b) turn down (*type 2*)   That music is very loud. Could you turn it down please? ✓

c) ask for (*type 3*)   They asked for some more chicken. ✓

d) go along with (*type 4*) He went along her idea with to grow vegetables in the garden. ✗

e) give back (*type 2*)   Are you going to give back it? ✗

f) take off (*type 1*)   The plane took it off three hours late. ✗

g) put on (*type 2*)   He put his trousers on very quickly. ✓

h) get in (*type 3*)   He got the bus in and sat down. ✗

i) pick up (*type 2*)   He picked up the pen and started writing. ✓

Picking Up

Learning a new language

Introductory Discussion Question

What different ways are there of learning a language?

Reading Task 1

Read the text on the next page quickly to answer these questions.

1 Where do you think the text comes from?
2 Who is the writer?
3 Who is s/he writing to?

Reading Text

...As for my Arabic...well, things are not going too badly. I feel I'm slowly **picking** it **up**. I go to classes every morning for an hour and a half. They are OK, but the teacher is very strict. He gets irritated if you make a mistake, so I just **shut up** and don't say anything, but I do take lots of notes. We do some speaking and a little writing every day and I'm gradually beginning to **work out** the difference between all the letters of the alphabet, though it's not easy. Some people in the class have studied Arabic before and they generally **catch on** much quicker than me when new things are introduced, but I try and do lots of homework and so I'm **keeping up** with the others OK.

The best thing though is just walking around town— people often ask you to come in their shop and have a cup of tea. Obviously I can't say much yet but it's a good chance for them to practise their English and for me to practise my Arabic. Somehow, between us, we can generally **get across** what we want to say.

It's funny but some words and expressions you hear again and again, like 'shokran' (which means 'thank you'). I try and make an effort to **find out** what new words mean, either by asking someone or by **looking** them **up** in my English /Arabic dictionary, and then learning them by heart.

All in all, I feel I'm able to **get by** in Arabic for the day-to-day things like shopping, catching buses and taxis, saying 'Hello' to people and so on.

My job, on the other hand, has not been going so well...

Reading Task 2

Read the text again and answer the following questions.

1 What different ways does the writer use to improve her/his Arabic?
2 Does s/he feel pleased with her/his progress in Arabic?

Focus on Phrasal Verbs

Find a phrasal verb in the text that means:

communicate = *get across* ...... (*type 2*)
survive = *get by* ...... (*type 1*)
discover = *find out* ...... (*type 2*)
keep quiet = *shut up* ...... (*type 1*) [informal]
learn = *pick up* ...... (*type 2*)
understand = *catch on* ...... (*type 1*)
maintain the same level = *keep up* ...... (*type 1*)
look for information in a reference book ...... (*type 2*) = *look up*
mentally calculate = *work out* ...... (*type 2*)

Controlled Practice

A Put the words in the correct order to make sentences. More
than one answer is possible in some cases.

Example:
was she she out angry when found very
When she found out she was very angry.

1 him up father to his told shut
2 up it you what it if know don't means look
3 difficult it across to was get idea the
4 Spanish on enough I've get got holiday to by
5 what he I out means work can't
6 catch I not saying they on could what to was
7 workers I up by job picked the watching the other
8 that him he keep so with fast can't walks I up

B Can you think of an appropriate way to end/begin what these
people are saying?

Example:
I have never been able to find out...*why the English drive on the
left-hand side of the road!*

1 I sometimes find it difficult to keep up...
2 I catch on quickly when...
3 I can't work out why...
4 ...and so I shut up!
5 ...and so I looked it up in a dictionary.
6 ...but I managed to get by.
7 ...but I couldn't get across what I meant.
8 ...and I picked it up very quickly.

Free Practice

Target language:
catch on/find out/get across/get by/keep up/look up/pick up/shut up/work out

---

Discuss with another student your experience of beginning to learn a new language – either English or possibly another language. Use the phrasal verbs from this unit as appropriate.

Ask and answer:

- what language it was
- why you were trying to learn it
- how you were trying to learn it (in a class, from books etc)
- what helped you the most to learn it
- if you had any particular difficulties
- if you liked learning it and why/why not
- what you think your level is in this language now and what you can do in it, for example, get by in everyday situations

Writing Task

Write a short text for foreigners coming to your country about the best way for them to pick up the language and how to get by in simple everyday situations.

"Well, really! You'd think by now he'd have picked up English."

Getting Through

2

Arranging a meeting

Introductory Discussion Questions

1 Why do you think people find speaking on the telephone in a
   foreign language especially difficult?
2 What phrases or expressions do you know in English which are
   particularly common/useful when speaking on the telephone?

Listening Task 1

Read the questions then listen to the cassette.

1 What does the person making the call want?
2 Does he get what he wants?

Listening Task 2

Listen to the cassette again and complete this summary of the
phone conversation.

John Stevens, who works for .... , phoned .... , who works for .... . He wanted
to change the date of their meeting originally arranged for .... because of .... .
They agreed a new date of .... but John still has to contact .... .

Focus on Phrasal Verbs

A There are nine phrasal verbs in the telephone conversation. Listen to the conversation again and put the following verbs and particles together as you hear them.

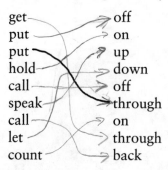

get   off
put   on
put   up
hold   down
call   off
speak   through
call   on
let   through
count   back

B Now, try and match them to the following meanings:

return the call	......	*call back*
wait	......	*hold on*
postpone	......	*put off*
connect	......	*put through*
cancel	......	*call off*
make contact	......	*get through*
fail/disappoint	......	*let down*
depend on	......	*count on*
talk louder	......	*speak up*

C Listen to nine extracts from the same conversation and write down exactly what you hear.

1 ....
2 ....
3 ....
4 ....
5 ....
6 ....
7 ....
8 ....
9 ....

Then decide from the context if each phrasal verb is:

Type 1 (verb + adverb [no object])
Type 2 (verb + adverb + object / verb + object + adverb)
Type 3 (verb + preposition + object)

NB. For more help on the different types of phrasal verb see pages xiii, xiv.

Controlled Practice

A Six of these sentences are grammatically possible, six are not. Find the incorrect sentences and correct them. The first one has been done for you.

Example:
1 I've been trying to get you through for ages but the line's always engaged!   NOT CORRECT.
*I've been trying to get through **to you** for ages but the line's always engaged!*

2 Please hold it on. Mr Jameson will be with you in a minute. ✗
3 Don't let down me. I really need your help this time.
4 Can you call back later, I'm rather busy at the moment? ✓
5 You can't call off the wedding now – we've sent out the invitations! ✓
6 Please call back me before this evening.
7 Do you mind if we put off coming until next weekend? ✓
8 You can never count on him. He's just unreliable. ✓
9 Is your phone broken? I can never seem to get you through. *to you*
10 Can you put me through to Mike for a quick word? ✓
11 Please speak it up, I can't hear you. ✗
12 If we let them down again, they will cancel the order. ✓

B In pairs, ask and answer these questions.

1 What would you do if you wanted to complain over the phone to the manager of an organisation but the secretary wouldn't put you through to her/him?
2 What do you do when someone tells you to hold on and you are still holding on five minutes later?
3 When would you ask someone to speak up?
4 If you had an important message for someone but you couldn't get through to them, what would you do?
5 Have you ever arranged an important event and then had to call it off? If so, why?
6 *Never put off until tomorrow what you can do today.*
What do you think of this saying?
7 Have you ever been seriously let down by a friend that you have been counting on? What happened?

Free Practice

Target language:
call back/call off/count on/get through/hold on/let down/put off/put through/
speak up

---

1 In groups of three try and act out the original conversation.
   Take it in turns to play each of the three roles. It's not necessary
   to keep *exactly* to the original script – feel free to invent.

2 Work in groups of three again. Decide who is Student A,
   Student B and Student C. Study the information given to you
   and prepare what you are going to say. Then act out the
   conversation. Try to use the phrasal verbs from this unit.

> **Student A.**
> You are an operator at PTC Ltd. The phones are very busy
> this morning and you often have to ask the callers if they
> would like to hold on, call back later or leave a message.

> **Student B.**
> You are Chris Davies. You work at Acwac Ltd. You supply
> PTC Ltd with office equipment. You had originally arranged
> a meeting with Pat Simmonds for two weeks ago to discuss a
> contract for next year, but s/he has put it off twice for
> different reasons. You have been trying to get through all day
> but s/he is always out or her/his line is busy. You have left
> messages but s/he hasn't called back. You are getting worried
> s/he doesn't want the meeting. Phone her/him and find out
> what is happening. Insist you speak to her/him.

> **Student C.**
> You are Pat Simmonds. You work for PTC Ltd. You usually
> buy the office equipment for your company from Acwac Ltd
> but you have been approached by another company who are
> going to make you an offer within two weeks. You want to
> know their offer before you meet Chris Davies of Acwac Ltd.

Writing Task

Write the dialogue of one of the above conversations.

Cracking Down!

The problem of violence at football matches

Introductory Discussion Questions

1 Do you have a problem with violence at football matches in your country?
2 Why do you think this is such a serious problem in some countries?

Reading Task 1

Read the text quickly to answer these questions.

1 Where do you think this text comes from?
2 Why did Mr Middleton write this text?

Reading Text

news that thousands of hours of television coverage
are helping to establish an audience dependent on a

Yours faithfully,
C. W. TURNBULL

Football hooliganism
From Mr R. J. Middleton

Sir, I am writing in response to H. Smith's letter of
18th June, complaining about the number of police at
football matches. Does he realise that violent crime
during and after games has *gone up* by 30% in the last
five years? If this level is to be *brought down*, then we
must support our police in their attempts to *crack
down* on violent behaviour, and not criticise them.

Why should people *get away with* anti-social and
even dangerous acts in the name of sport? Our
football supporters are *coming in for* a lot of criticism
worldwide and other governments are beginning to

look into the possibility of stopping our clubs playing
in their countries. We shouldn't *rule out* the possibility of stricter punishments for football hooligans;
if a few examples were made and the people respon-
sible were *put away* for a long time, we might earn the
respect of other countries. If we continue to *let*
hooligans *off* lightly, then we may have to *do away
with* the idea of international matches completely.

It is easy to criticise the police for ruining sports
events, but we must remember who is really re-
sponsible — the hooligans.

Yours faithfully,
R. J. MIDDLETON

Monetary union
From Ms Helen Wilkes

the European Commission's reluctance partly dem-
onstrates the difficulty with which the British gov-

Reading Task 2

Read the text again and answer the following questions.

1 What does Mr Middleton think the consequence of the problem
of football hooliganism might be?
2 What does he suggest should be done about the problem?

Focus on Phrasal Verbs

From the context in the letter, can you suggest the approximate
meaning of each of the phrasal verbs.

go up	...... (*type 1*)	look into	...... (*type 3*)
bring down	...... (*type 2*)	rule out	...... (*type 2*)
crack down	...... (*type 1*)	put away	...... (*type 2*)
get away with	...... (*type 4*)	let off	...... (*type 2*)
come in for	...... (*type 4*)	do away with	...... (*type 4*)

Controlled Practice

A Match up the halves of these sentences.

Example: 1c)
If the number of violent crimes goes up any higher we shall have to introduce capital punishment.

1 If the number of violent crimes goes up any higher
2 Someone who commits murder
3 He was very lucky
4 If we don't do away with this system
5 We must look into ways of
6 They only steal because
7 We are going to crack down
8 We haven't ruled out

a) we are going to come in for a great deal of criticism.
b) the idea of Community Service for minor criminals.
c) we shall have to introduce capital punishment.
d) they think they can get away with it.
e) should be put away for life.
f) on all forms of terrorism.
g) to be let off with a fine.
h) bringing down the level of violence at football matches.

B Replace the words in *italics* with one of the phrasal verbs you saw in the letter. Change the form of the phrasal verb as necessary.

Example:
Why do you think he *got* so much criticism for releasing them from prison?
Why do you think he **came in for** *so much criticism for releasing them from prison?*

1 We can't *stop* evening visiting at the prison – there would be a riot!
2 You need to *examine* exactly why these young people become football hooligans.
3 The number of people in prison has been *increasing* steadily over the last ten years.
4 He has been *sent to prison* for six months.
5 I am sure the judge will *not punish you*.
6 We can't *dismiss* the idea of a bigger police force.
7 If we don't *take strong measures* these people will take over our society.
8 It's incredible how vandals destroy property like this and *are not punished for* it.
9 We are trying to *reduce* the numbers of people in prison.

Free Practice

Target language:
bring down/come in for/crack down/do away with/get away with/go up/let off/
look into/put away/rule out

Discuss with other students what you think of R J Middleton's
ideas. What ideas do *you* have for reducing football hooliganism?

Writing Task

Write a letter to the same newspaper responding to
R J Middleton's letter.

Getting On

4

Relationship problems

Introductory Discussion Question

What different reasons do people have for finishing relationships?

Listening Task 1

Read the questions then listen to the cassette.

1 What are the names of the people in the relationship you hear discussed?
2 What is their problem?
3 Does it finish their relationship?

Listening Task 2

Now listen again and decide if the following statements are **true** or **false**.

1 Mike and Julie have been together for more than twelve months.
2 Three different things made Julie suspicious.
3 Mike said that he loved both Julie and Patricia.
4 Julie immediately told Mike she was going to leave him.
5 Mike and Julie are together at the moment.

Focus on Phrasal Verbs

Listen again to the original conversation and see if you can hear one phrasal verb for each of these meanings.

have a (romantic) relationship	...... (*type 1*)
have a good relationship with someone	...... (*type 1*)
happen	...... (*type 1*)
pretend	...... (*type 1*)
deceive	...... (*type 2*)
tolerate	...... (*type 4*)
agree to someone else's demands	...... (*type 1*)
recover from	...... (*type 3*)
finish a relationship and separate	...... (*type 1*)

Controlled Practice

1 Complete this text with one phrasal verb in each space.

> Amanda and Kevin got married five years ago. They had been ...(a)...for about two years before that. However, a friend of Amanda's saw Kevin with another woman in a restaurant and told Amanda. When Kevin told her nothing was wrong and that the woman was just a business client, Amanda was ...(b)... . However, Kevin kept having to go away on business trips and once or twice Amanda answered the phone and the person at the other end put the phone down without speaking.
> She asked Kevin what was ...(c)... . He ...(d)...that he didn't know what she was talking about. She didn't accept that and insisted he told her the truth. Finally, he told her everything. Amanda decided to ...(e)...the situation for the sake of the children but later changed her mind and said she was going to leave him. He begged her to stay and eventually she ...(f)... . That was only about a year ago but they seem to have ...(g)... it now. They are ...(h)...very well with each other and I doubt very much that they will ...(i)... .

2 List the differences between the above text about Amanda and Kevin and the one on the cassette about Julie and Mike.

Free Practice

Target language:
get on/get over/give in/go on/go out/make out/put up with/split up/take in

1 Discuss the following questions:
   a) What would you do in Julie's situation?
   b) Do you think a couple can get over a crisis like this?

2 Look at these pictures. Put them in a possible order and prepare
   a story which links them all, trying to incorporate as many of
   the different phrasal verbs in this unit as possible.

a)

b)

c)

d)

e)

f)

Now, tell your story to other students in your class.

Writing Task

Write up your story or **one** of the stories that you heard told by
another group.

5

Cutting Back

Company success and failure

Introductory Discussion Question

What different reasons can you think of for companies:

a) doing well?
b) doing badly?

Reading Task 1

Read the text quickly to answer these questions.

1 Is Hitec doing well at the moment?
2 Is Electrix doing well at the moment?

Reading Text

… and raw material costs have *shot up* during the last year. It is not surprising then that Hitec Ltd has decided to *cut back* on its Manchester workforce. It is estimated that 15% of the 6,500 men and women employed will have to be *laid off*. Another result is that it has *pulled out* of the American market completely and concentrated on Western Europe. However, apparently plans to *get round* unfavourable new laws by opening factories in Belgium and Germany have been **put off** for a further six months. It appears that rumours that it was going to *take over* Connex Ltd are not true. Unless they can *come up with* some radical ideas to improve the situation it doesn't look like things are going to *pick up* in the coming year.

On the other hand, since the beginning of the year, sales at Electrix plc have *taken off* due to the development of some exciting new models. In fact it seems they are having trouble **keeping up** with production requirements. However, not everything is going well at Electrix — the deal with Formatco has *fallen through* because they could not agree on certain key issues of design.

… can improve their performance in the coming financial year, then they will … making for a more representative breakdown of costs incurred to date,

Reading Task 2

Read the text again and answer the following questions.

1 What are the reasons for the success and failure of each company?
2 What are the consequences of the difficulties at Hitec?
3 What problems has Electrix had?

Focus on Phrasal Verbs

Look at the phrasal verbs in the article and choose the correct meaning for each one.

1 shoot up (*type 1*)   = ~~increase a little~~/increase a lot
2 cut back (*type 1*)   = increase/reduce
3 lay off (*type 2*)   = sack/give jobs
4 pull out (*type 1*)   = withdraw from/enter
5 get round (*type 3*)   = meet/avoid
6 take over (*type 2*)   = work together with/take control of
7 pick up (*type 1*)   = get better/get worse
8 take off (*type 1*)   = begin to increase dramatically/stop
                             increasing
9 fall through (*type 1*) = continue as planned/not happen

Controlled Practice

A Some of the phrasal verbs in these sentences can be used in the passive and keep the original meaning of the sentence. Decide which can be put into the passive and change the sentence appropriately.

Example:
Frenlink Inc has not *taken over* Carrods Ltd.
Carrods Ltd has not **been taken over** *by Frenlink Inc.*

1 His trainer *pulled* him *out* of the competition at the last minute because of problems with his leg.
2 The number of students coming to the school *shot up* last year.
3 At the last minute the deal *fell through*.
4 They are going to *lay off* a number of administrative staff as a result of a massive reorganisation programme.
5 We can't *cut back* on the number of nurses!
6 It's incredible. Sales of the book have *taken off*.
7 We must *get round* this problem. Perhaps we could ask your father's advice.
8 If business doesn't *pick up*, we will need a loan from the bank.

B Look at this advertisement and find the phrasal verb!

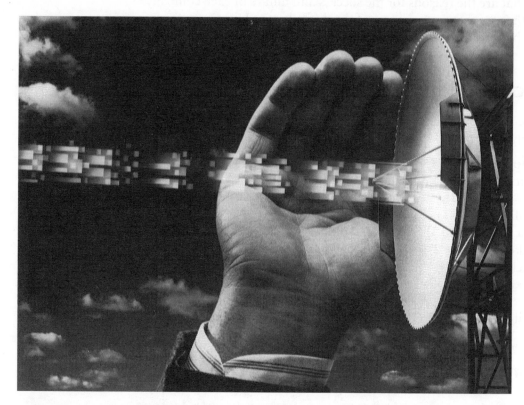

You wouldn't believe how much this man's business is picking up.

A year ago, he was watching his company's competitive edge being steadily eroded.

More and more rivals seemed to be making the same products, for the same market, at the same price.

A pretty unspeakable situation.

Unspeakable that is, until he started talking British Telecom's Language of Business.

Of course, things didn't change overnight.

They changed in seconds. Because that's how long it took to start receiving information using our fax machines, telex and data networks.

Market information he never even knew existed before.

Thanks to British Telecom's electronic mail service, letters could be received in one minute and responded to in the next.

Whilst our public data network enabled his branch offices, production line and stock warehouse to talk to each other instantaneously.

So cutting out manufacturing inefficiency and allowing for guaranteed delivery dates.

A year later, he's not the only one delighted with the situation. His customers are too.

In fact, using his 0800 number, they can ring and compliment him on the improved service. At no cost to themselves.

If you'd like to know what British Telecom could do for your company's competitive edge, call us free on 0800 800 856 or cut out the coupon.

That is, if one of your rivals hasn't snipped it out already.

CALL ☎ FREE 0800 800 856 ANYTIME

Please send me the British Telecom Business Catalogue and Action Pack.

Title Mr/Mrs/Miss _____ Initials _____

Surname _____

Job Title _____

Telephone Code _____ No. _____

Company Name _____

Company Address _____

_____ Postcode _____

British Telecom, Department ASL, FREEPOST 800, Bristol BS1 6GZ.
No stamp needed.

British
TELECOM
It's you we answer to

C Make appropriate answers for these questions using the phrasal verbs in brackets.

Example:
What are you going to do about your low profits this year? (cut back)
One thing we are going to do is **cut back** *on the number of administrative staff.*

1 What happened to sales of colour TVs in the first part of the year? (shoot up)
2 Why are you looking so depressed? What's happened? (lay off)
3 Is John still going to play in the match on Saturday? (pull out)
4 Won't your father stop you coming to the party? (get round)
5 What do you think IBN is going to do next? (take over)
6 How's life at the moment? (pick up)
7 You are looking happy! Why? (take off)
8 Are you still going to sell your car to that guy you met last week? (fall through)

Free Practice

Target language:
cut back/fall through/get round/lay off/pick up/pull out/shoot up/take off/take over

The Personnel Manager and the Union representative meet to discuss working conditions. Work in pairs. Decide who is Student A and who is Student B. Study the information given to you and prepare what you are going to say. Then act out the conversation. Try to use the phrasal verbs from this unit where possible.

Student A.
You are the Personnel Manager of a company. You are going to meet with a Union representative. Your company must cut back on the number of people it employs. Explain to the Union representative:
- why this needs to be done (for example, inflation, high interest rates, competition etc)
- what is going to happen (for example, reorganisation in the company, changes of responsibility for the people who stay etc)
- how this will benefit the company in the long term (for example, the company may survive, better profits, increased wages, better work conditions etc)

> **Student B.**
> You are a Union representative. You have been called to a meeting with the Personnel Manager of your company. You have heard rumours that some members of your Union are going to be laid off. You are definitely not going to allow this to happen. You are also quite angry because management promised a 10% increase in salary and improved working conditions for the workforce six weeks ago and still nothing has happened.

Writing Task

Either write:

A an account for the Board of Directors of your company of what happened in your meeting with the Union representative.

OR

B an account for the members of your Union of what happened in your meeting with the Personnel Manager.

Revision One

Mistake Search

A Listen to the story and put the pictures in the correct order.

a)

b)

c)

d)

e)

f)

B Now read the story. In each of the nine phrasal verbs, the particle (or one of the particles) is wrong. Correct the incorrect particles.

On Friday morning at 8.00am Brian Hawkins went to work as usual. He walked to the underground station, waited a few minutes for his train on the crowded platform, and then got on. As usual he had to **put up from** standing the whole way.

At Victoria, where a large numbers of passengers always change, Brian felt someone push past him aggressively. It was a tall, well-dressed young man. At first Brian couldn't **work up** what was happening and then he felt for his wallet. To his horror, he realised it wasn't there and it had all his credit cards plus over £100 in cash. Brian couldn't believe that he had been **taken off** by such an old trick. He was furious. He certainly wasn't going to let this guy **get away by** it that easily.

He tried to **find up** where the young man had gone. Finally he saw him on the platform. He ran out of the train, grabbed the man and pulled him back towards the train. The man tried to **make off** that he didn't know what was **going through**.

Brian jumped back into the train just as the doors were closing. The doors shut on the young man's coat, trapping him. A look of panic crossed his face as the train started to move. The train slowly accelerated and the young man had to run to **keep down** with the train. Just as the train was leaving the station and the young man was about to come off the end of the platform, he pulled himself away from the train and fell backwards onto the platform.

That evening, when Brian got back home, he was just about to tell his wife the whole story, when she asked him how he had managed to **get down** without any money.

'What do you mean?' Brian asked.
'Well, you left your wallet here on the kitchen table when you went to work this morning.'

Phrasal Verb Square

A There are nine phrasal verbs in this square. They all come from
Units 1–5. They can be read horizontally, vertically or
diagonally. Individual letters may be used in more than one
phrasal verb. The first one has been done for you.

K	O	L	A	Y	O	F	F	S
E	A	S	O	T	F	I	P	E
E	J	T	H	O	N	U	L	L
P	R	A	T	U	K	E	L	E
U	L	U	R	A	T	U	E	T
P	P	N	E	A	Y	U	P	D
R	E	P	I	C	K	U	P	O
T	S	P	L	I	T	U	P	W
Q	U	E	S	H	O	G	I	N

B Now insert each of the phrasal verbs into one of these sentences
as appropriate.

1 I'm sure he won't .... you .... . He always does what he says.
2 Tell her to .... ! I'm trying to work.
3 It took me a long time to .... any Japanese. It's a very
   difficult language.
4 They are going to .... 300 workers at the local factory.
5 I'm not surprised they .... They had nothing in common.
6 Can you .... ? I can't hear anything you are saying.
7 You mustn't .... going to the doctor's any longer. The
   problem will only get worse.
8 When I read an article in English, I only .... the difficult
   words when I've read it once completely.
9 I can't .... with the other students. I think I will change
   classes.

Student Competition

A Work in teams. (There must be at least three teams.) Each team prepares some sentences with words which can be replaced by a phrasal verb from Units 1–5.

Example:
They *cancelled* the match because of the weather.
Answer: *called off*

B Each team in turn shows a sentence to the other teams. The other teams try to give the correct phrasal verb. The first team to give the correct answer scores a point. The winning team is the one with the most points after an agreed number of rounds.

"They've always got on wonderfully together."

Pulling Through

6

Illness

Introductory Discussion Questions

1 How do you feel about going to the doctor's?
2 What are the characteristics of a good doctor?
3 What do you think of the health system in your country?

Listening Task 1

Read the questions then listen to the cassette.

1 Why does the patient go to see the doctor?
2 What does the doctor recommend?

Listening Task 2

Now listen again and answer the following questions.

1 What happened to Mrs Barrett's mother?
2 What's wrong with Mrs Barrett's arm?
3 Who helped Mrs Barrett when she felt ill yesterday afternoon?
4 How many other people have had the same kind of problem recently?
5 What kind of job does Mrs Barrett have?

Focus on Phrasal Verbs

A Listen to the conversation again and match up the following
phrasal verbs with their appropriate meaning:

pull through (*type 1*)
lay up (*type 2*)*
come out in (*type 4*)
pass out (*type 1*)
come down with (*type 4*)

wear out (*type 2*)
take (time) off (*type 2*)
carry out (*type 2*)

catch (a virus/disease)
do
lose consciousness
make very tired
cause to stay in bed (as a result of
accident/illness)
be all right, survive
show the signs of illness
spend time doing something different
from your usual work

*generally used in the passive

B Describe what is happening in each of these pictures using the
phrasal verbs above.

a)

b)

c)

d)

e)

f)

Controlled Practice

A Imagine a situation in which each of the following sentences might have been said and then create a short dialogue around it.

Example:
Do you think he'll pull through?

Possible situation = *someone has just had a heart attack – relatives are asking the doctor about the patient's condition.*

Possible dialogue = *– How is he doctor?*
– Well. . .he has had a slight heart attack.
– Yes, but, do you think he will pull through?
– Oh yes. He'll be fine eventually, but for the moment he just needs lots of rest and quiet.

1 And, do you know, I was laid up for six months!
2 And all the children came out in these strange red spots.
3 One minute he was standing there. The next he had passed out.
4 Excuse me, sir. We are carrying out a survey on attitudes to the national health system.
5 I hope you don't come down with it as well.
6 I can't. I'm absolutely worn out.
7 Do you think he'll let me take a few days off?

B There is one mistake in each of these sentences. What is it?

Example:
He laid up for three weeks with a badly broken foot last month.
He *was* laid up for three weeks with a badly broken foot last month.

1 He's rather tired now. The children wore out with all their questions.
2 First he come out in spots, and then he became very hot and feverish.
3 I'm not surprised he passed out it after drinking all that beer.
4 I took two weeks of in July.
5 We all came down in flu over Christmas.
6 If I don't pull it through, will you take care of the children?
7 He's like a dictator. I am apparently just here to carry up his orders.

Free Practice

Target language:
carry out/come down with/come out in/lay up/pass out/pull through/
take (time) off/wear out

Work in groups of three or four. Take it in turns to take the role of
Student A. Try to use the phrasal verbs from this unit where
possible.

Student A.
The doctor has called to say he has a temperature and can't
come in today. You are a nurse in the doctor's surgery. See
the different patients who are waiting and offer advice as
necessary.

Student B/C/D.
You are patients. Decide on your particular symptoms and
then go and see the doctor for advice.

Writing Task

Imagine you and some friends have gone on holiday to another
country. Unfortunately, the holiday is a disaster! You and your
friends have one accident/illness after another. Write a letter to a
friend describing the holiday using the phrasal verbs from this
unit.

Giving Away

Winning a fortune

Introductory Discussion Questions

1 What would you do if you won £2,000,000?
2 Would you save it, give it away or spend it?
   Or do a little of each?

Reading Task 1

Read the text quickly to answer this question.

Did winning the money make the couple happier in the end?

Reading Text

Up until a year ago, Arthur and Mildred Watkins were just a very ordinary middle-aged couple. They lived in a small suburb, just outside Birmingham. With two teenage children and a large mortgage, life wasn't easy. And then disaster struck . . . Arthur lost his job. Mildred remembers what happened:

*Arthur just couldn't find another job. He was too old, you see. Soon we had **fallen behind** with mortgage payments and they **cut** the phone **off** as we couldn't pay the bill. We had to borrow money from the bank, from friends . . . it was awful! It began to really **get me down**. Arthur began drinking a lot. I just didn't know what to do.*

And then the incredible happened . . . Arthur continues the story:

We got this letter — official-looking it was. I thought it was going to be another demand from the bank, but it wasn't. It was a letter telling us we had won £2,000,000.

From that day Arthur and Mildred's life changed completely. But not all for the good.

The first thing they did was to *settle up* all their debts. Then they bought a large Rolls-Royce and several fur coats for Mildred. They moved down south and bought a large luxury flat in the middle of the West End of London. They flew on Concorde to the States,

went around the casinos in Las Vegas and stayed in all the big hotels.

*Our big mistake was not planning what to do with the money. We never **put** any **by**. I suppose we just went a bit mad. As well as that, a lot of people wrote to us, telling us about of all their problems and why they needed money. So we **gave away** a lot of money. We wanted to help.*

Another problem arose when they were visited by a certain Mr James Harkington. Mr Harkington introduced himself as a 'professional investment consultant' . . .

*That Harkington man — he really **ripped** us **off**. He looked so respectable and told us how we had to invest our money carefully for the future. Anyway, we agreed to buy shares in some company in Manchester. After just four weeks we heard it was out of business and we had lost all our money. Harkington had disappeared.*

And now. . . the money has nearly all gone. Arthur and Mildred are trying to sell their London flat and move back to Birmingham but things aren't looking good.

*None of our friends want to see us now, they all say we are too good for them now. Things just can't **go on** like this but I just don't know what we are going to do.*

Reading Task 2

Read the text again and answer the following questions.

1 What different problems did the couple have *before* they won the money?
2 What different problems did the couple have *after* they won the money?

Focus on Phrasal Verbs

Find a phrasal verb in the text that means:

save	...... (*type 2*)
continue	...... (*type 1*)
cheat	...... (*type 2*) [informal]
be late	...... (*type 1*)
distribute	...... (*type 2*)
depress	...... (*type 2*)*
disconnect	...... (*type 2*)
pay back	...... (*type 1*)

* The object never goes after the particle 'down'.

Controlled Practice

A Match the halves of the dialogue.

Example: 1d)
Can we settle up at the end of the week? Sure, whenever you've got the money.

1 Can we settle up at the end of the week?
2 Why do you never seem to have any money these days?
3 What's the matter? Why are you looking so angry?
4 Why don't we give away those old chairs?
5 Did you really sell him that antique table for only £20?
6 Are you and John still arguing a lot?
7 What will happen if he goes on being late for work?
8 Why do you want the money?

a) Who to? No-one would want them.
b) Yes. It's really beginning to get me down.
c) I have fallen behind with the rent again and the landlord said if we don't pay we'll have to go.
d) Sure, whenever you've got the money.
e) He'll probably get the sack.

f) They have just cut off the gas and electricity but I paid all the bills.

g) I'm trying to put by as much as I can so that we can buy a new car.

h) Why? Do you think he ripped me off?

B Complete the following gaps with one of the phrasal verbs above in the correct form.

Example:
When we didn't pay the telephone bill, we *were cut off*.

1 If you .... working like this, you will have a heart attack!
2 It's easy to be .... when you buy a secondhand car.
3 He has been unemployed for more than a year. It's really .... him .... .
4 I promise I'll .... when I get my next pay cheque.
5 He decided to .... all his money and go and work with the poor in Calcutta.
6 When we .... with payments for our new car, they sent someone to take it back.
7 I am trying to .... a little money .... each month to give my grandchildren, when they are a little older.

Free Practice

Target language:
cut off/fall behind/get down/give away/go on/put by/rip off/settle up

Prepare to tell the story of Arnold and Mabel, a couple very similar to Arthur and Mildred who were very poor but who also won £2,000,000. Arnold and Mabel had a fantastic time with the money and are now much happier as a result.

When you are ready, tell your story to another student.

Writing Task

Write up the story you prepared.

8 Breaking Down

A difficult journey

Introductory Discussion Questions

1 Are you generally on time for things?
2 How do you feel when other people arrive late?
3 If you agreed to meet someone in the middle of town and they weren't there at the agreed time, how long would you wait for them? And then what would you do?

Listening Task 1

Read the question then listen to the cassette.

Did Steve and John arrive late because:

a) of the weather?
b) lots of things went wrong on the way?
c) they went to another friend's birthday party first?

Listening Task 2

Listen to the cassette again and decide what different reasons Steve and John have for being late.

Focus on Phrasal Verbs

Listen to nine extracts from the dialogue. Each one contains a
phrasal verb. Write down exactly what you hear and then decide
what the phrasal verb means in the context given.

1 .... (*type 1*)
2 .... (*type 2*)
3 .... (*type 1*)
4 .... (*type 2*)
5 .... (*type 1*)
6 .... (*type 2*)
7 .... (*type 2*)
8 .... (*type 2*)
9 .... (*type 1*)

Controlled Practice

A Make complete and grammatical sentences from the prompts.

Example:
We/set off/tomorrow/week's holiday/Wales.
We are setting off tomorrow for a week's holiday in Wales.

1 I/pick you up/station/8.30pm tomorrow evening.
2 He/fill up/car/before/they go/the journey yesterday.
3 John, we/run out/milk/again!/That is/third time/this week.
4 Look!/large black car/pull up/in front/our house.
5 We/hold up/several hours/the airport/because of/bomb scare.
6 He promised/make up/lost time/working/his holidays.
7 I/never/actually/run anybody over/but/I/do/once/hit/cyclist.
8 If/car/break down again/I/sell it!

B Answer these questions using the phrasal verbs in brackets.

Example:
Do you have any problems with your car? (break down)
Generally no, but it sometimes breaks down in very cold weather.

1 Why are you so late? (hold up)
2 Is there any petrol in the car? (fill up)
3 How are you going to get home after the party? (pick up)
4 How are you going to get to London by 10am? (make up)
5 What are you looking at? (pull up)
6 I thought you said you were going to be late. You're the first one
  to arrive. (set off)
7 Have you ever had an accident? (run over)
8 Have you got any more orange juice? (run out)

Free Practice

Target language:
break down/fill up/hold up/make up/pick up/pull up/run out/run over/set off

---

Have you ever been on a disastrous car journey?
Prepare to talk about one, either real or imaginary.

- Spend a few minutes thinking about what you are going to say.
- Provide as much detail as possible. Remember to include any phrasal verbs from this or other units that are appropriate.

Now, tell your story to another student.

Writing Task

With a composition entitled *One of those days!* Write between 120 and 180 words and include at least six phrasal verbs.

"Is it cheaper to fill up with litres or gallons?"

Taking After

9

Family relationships

Introductory Discussion Questions

What different kinds of problems can exist between children and their parents? Why do you think these problems occur?

Reading Task 1

Read the text on the next page quickly to answer this question.

What do you think is the relationship of the two people to John?

Reading Text

'Do you think John *takes after* his father?' she asked quietly.

At first Maureen wasn't sure what to say.

'In what way do you mean?'

'Well, you know... his character, his personality. I mean, they do both seem so incredibly stubborn ...' She paused. 'You know, I'm sure, how much John *looks up to* his Dad ...'

'Yes, I know.' Maureen felt sad.

'... but at the same time his Dad is always *putting* him *down*. He doesn't take him seriously. I think it really depresses John. I mean, he's doing so well in his job at the moment but his father never says anything about it.'

Maureen was surprised by the force of Sarah's feeling. She had never heard her speak so strongly about anything before. She wanted to explain.

'Yes, I know, but his father doesn't take dance seriously. I know it really **gets** John **down**. He won't even go and watch John perform. He never did.' Her mind went back to the difficult years.

'Actually, it was just the same when John was *growing up*. I remember he always used to *show off* in front of his Dad, but Bill would never pay any attention to him. In fact it was generally difficult ... *bringing up* John. His father never took any interest.'

'But Maureen ... John won't admit it hurts. He tries to **make out** that he doesn't care. But I know he still *keeps on* trying ... trying to *live up to* some image of the perfect son. I just don't understand.'

Maureen felt sorry for the younger woman's frustration — she understood it very well.

'Well, you see, Bill was always disappointed that John didn't go into the family business.'

'What! John a builder!'

'Yes I know it sounds ridiculous. Of course it would be the wrong thing for John but Bill always had this picture of them working side by side, father and son. I remember him talking about when he would change the name of the firm to 'Henderson and Son'. And then when John refused to go to the Technical College and *took up* dance seriously ... well, Bill never really forgave him.'

Sarah was outraged.

'But look. This can't go on. Bill has to understand that John has his own life to lead, his own needs ...'

248

Reading Task 2

Read the text again and then summarise the basic problem between John and his father.

Focus on Phrasal Verbs

1 Look at each of the phrasal verbs in the context of the above extract and say what you think they mean approximately.

take after ...... (*type 3*)   bring up ...... (*type 2*)
look up to ...... (*type 4*)   keep on ...... (*type 1*)
put down ...... (*type 2*)   live up to ...... (*type 4*)
grow up ...... (*type 1*)   take up ...... (*type 2*)
show off ...... (*type 1*)

Controlled Practice

A Someone/ Something?
a) Most of the above phrasal verbs are generally used in relation to people or things. With reference to their meanings in this unit, decide if they can be used with *someone, something*, both of these or neither of these.

Example:
to take after...*someone*

b) Now decide the appropriate position of *someone/something*.

Example:
to take after someone but NOT ~~to take someone after.~~

B Look at the following sentences and decide on the possible positions of the phrases/words in brackets.

Example:
He often puts down   (women/them)
– *He often puts down women.*
– *He often puts women down.*
– *He often puts them down.*

1 She says he takes after   (his father/him)
2 I am going to take up   (golf/it)
3 She always shows off in front of   (new people/them)
4 I remember when she was growing up   (Julie/her)
5 If he keeps on playing I am going to get angry   (that music/it)
6 It wasn't easy to bring up on my own   (a young son/him)
7 Do you think he will live up to?   (his reputation/it)
8 He looked up to because she was so clever   (his sister/her)

Free Practice

Target language:
bring up/grow up/keep on/live up to/look up to/put down/show off/take after/
take up

Sarah decides to go and see Bill to talk about the problem. In pairs,
act out the conversation that takes place between them. Try to use
the phrasal verbs from this unit.

> **Student A.**
> You are Bill, the father. Explain to Sarah how you feel about
> your relationship with your son.

> **Student B.**
> You are Sarah, the daughter-in-law. Explain to Bill how you
> feel about the problems between him and John.

Writing Task

Write the dialogue that took place between Bill and Sarah.

Blowing Up

10

The News

Introductory Discussion Question

Did you hear or read the news today or yesterday?
Discuss with other students the most important items in the news
at the moment.

Listening Task 1

Read the questions then listen to the cassette.

1 How many stories are there in this News programme?
2 What is the main subject of each?

Listening Task 2

Now listen again and decide if these statements are **true or false**.

1 Three people have been hurt in bomb explosions today.
2 The animals in the laboratories were not in good condition.
3 Members of Greenpeace were demonstrating against pollution
   of the environment today.
4 Liverpool has won the FA Cup final against Manchester United.
5 Mr J Arkwright has discovered some drawings by Picasso.

Focus on Phrasal Verbs

Listen to the news again. Put together the verbs and particles you hear mentioned and then match them to the appropriate meaning below.

A go ————————— off
blow   down
break   up
let   off
put   out
give   into
pull   up
come   out
clear   across

B

enter illegally	...... (*type 3*)
destroy with an explosive device	...... (*type 2*)
kill	...... (*type 2*)
find by chance	...... (*type 3*)
distribute	...... (*type 2*)
put in order	...... (*type 2*)
achieve	...... (*type 2*)
explode	...... (*type 1*)
free	...... (*type 2*)

Controlled Practice

A In some of these sentences *it* is missing. Other sentences are complete. Put in *it* where possible and where appropriate.

Example:
John's going to sleep in the spare bedroom, so I must clear up this afternoon.
*John's going to sleep in the spare bedroom, so I must clear **it** up this afternoon.*

1 The terrorists blew up last night.
2 To their horror, it didn't go off.
3 They broke into as soon as it was dark.
4 You must let out! It's cruel to keep an animal in such a small space.
5 The vet said should be put down.
6 I'll give out the homework at the end of the lesson.
7 It's incredible – they've pulled off again.
8 I came across this morning. It was behind my desk.

B For those sentences where you put in an *it* – what could or does the *it* refer to?

C Now make appropriate answers for these questions using the phrasal verbs in the brackets.

Example:
Why are all those people running out of that shop? (go off)
A bomb is going to go off in a minute.

1 What happened to that plane? (blow up)
2 Why are the police here? (break into)
3 Where are the mice you kept in that cage? (let out)
4 Your dog is very old now, isn't he? (put down)
5 What are all these people doing? (give out)
6 What do you think his chances are of winning the competition?
   (pull off)
7 I thought you said you had lost that ring? (come across)
8 What are you doing at the weekend? (clear up)

Free Practice

Target language:
blow up/break into/clear up/come across/give out/go off/let out/pull off/put down

Prepare another 9 o'clock News programme. If possible, try and imagine what tonight's news will be. Present your News items to the other students. Use as many of the phrasal verbs in this unit as possible and bring in phrasal verbs from other units if appropriate.

"Your wife wants to know if you'll agree
to have him put down."

Writing Task

Write a Summary section of the stories you have heard for a newspaper, like the one below from *The Independent*. Use as many phrasal verbs as possible.

SUMMARY

Murder plot

A detective was jailed for six years for plotting to murder his lover's husband
.... **Page 4**

Booker list

Works by Beryl Bainbridge, A S Byatt, Penelope Fitzgerald, John McGahern, Brian Moore, and Mordecai Richler are on the short list for the Booker Prize .... **Page 7**

Racial bias

One in five accommodation agencies discriminate against ethnic minorities, an inquiry shows .... **Page 7**

German-Soviet pact

United Germany has concluded its first treaty, committing it to friendly ties with the Soviet Union ... **Page 10**

Unemployment up

Unemployment rose by 22,300 last month to 1,654,000. Economists said 40,000 to 50,000 jobs a month could be lost by the spring as a result of the high interest rate policy ...... **Page 20**

Revision Two

Multiple Choice

Complete each of the following sentences with the appropriate phrasal verb.

1 It's not easy to .... small children as a single parent.
   a) grow up
   b) bring up
   c) take after
   d) live up to

2 I'm .... ! I didn't realise that cleaning the house would be such hard work.
   a) weared up
   b) wore out
   c) worn up
   d) worn out

3 I'll .... John up from the station at 5.00pm.
   a) pass
   b) take
   c) pick
   d) pull

4 If we .... with the payments again, they will take the car back.
   a) fall down
   b) fall behind
   c) fall back
   d) fall up

5 We must .... the house before the visitors arrive.
   a) clear up
   b) make up
   c) take up
   d) settle up

6 The News is always about disaster. It .... me down.
   a) gets
   b) takes
   c) pulls
   d) puts

7 The electricity was .... between 3.00pm and 9.00pm.
   a) pulled off
   b) set off
   c) take off
   d) cut off

8 We were .... in traffic for hours because of roadworks.
   a) hold on
   b) held on
   c) held up
   d) hold up

9 After the accident he was .... in bed for six months.
   a) pulled through
   b) got down
   c) laid up
   d) broken down

10 I must go to the shops. We've .... of bread.
   a) run out
   b) run behind
   c) ran out
   d) run over

Phrasal Verbs Crossword

Use the clues to help you complete this puzzle. The answers are all phrasal verbs from the last five units.

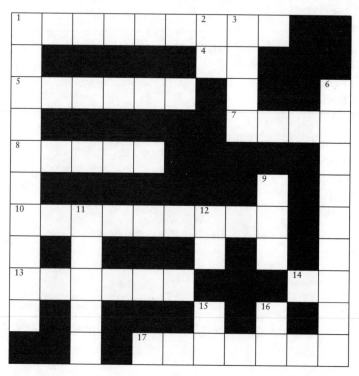

ACROSS

1 Peter's .... spots and he's got a temperature. Shall we call the doctor? (4,3,2)
4 If we go .... like this, we won't have any money left! (2)
5 He .... for being late by working an extra hour. (4,2)
7 Watch out! You nearly ran .... that cat. (4)
8 She takes .... her mother; always ready to help other people. (5)
10 I paid more than £100. Do you think I was .... ? (6,3)
13 Leave, depart. (3,3)
14 The bomb will .... off at exactly 12.00pm. (2)
17 Don't .... me .... ! I'm just as clever as you are. (3,4)

DOWN

1 Find by chance. (4,6)
2 Jane's got a lot to live up .... . Her sister was good at school. (2)
3 Someone has broken .... our flat. The stereo and TV have gone. (4)
6 If those computers .... again, I'm going to change the system. (5,4)
9 I may take some time .... at Christmas. It's a long time since I last had a holiday. (3)
11 I .... a little money each month in case of emergencies. (3,2)
12 If they keep .... making that noise, I'll call the police. (2)
15 Fill .... up, please. (2)
16 You know how he looks up .... you. He thinks you are fantastic! (2)

Student Competition

1 Work in small groups.
2 Decide on a subject to discuss. It can be anything, for example, *families, pollution, holidays, money* etc.
3 Write down five phrasal verbs from the last five units on five separate pieces of paper.
4 Give the five pieces of paper to the person on your left.
5 Each person will now have five phrasal verbs.
6 The object of the game is to discuss the subject and use the phrasal verbs you have been given.
7 Each time you use one of the phrasal verbs on your pieces of paper, put the paper with phrasal verb down in the middle of the table. (The other students/teacher will decide if you have used the phrasal verb correctly). When you use one of your phrasal verbs, your contribution to the discussion must follow reasonably naturally from the previous contribution.
8 The winner is the person to put all their phrasal verbs in the middle of the table first.

11 Moving In

Moving house/country

Introductory Discussion Question

What different things do you have to do when you want to move house?

Reading Task 1

Read the letter quickly to answer these questions.

1 Are Dee and Jeff positive or negative about their new situation?
2 Why do you think this?

Reading Text

> 1441 Baker Street,
> San Francisco,
> California,
> 94115 USA.
> 3rd October, 91
>
> Dear Jon and Trish,
>
> Hi! How are things? How's life with the new baby? I hope Jon's doing his share of the nappy-changing!
>
> I can hardly believe how long we've been out here now. As you know we got here at the beginning of August and are now really beginning to **settle in**. It was quite difficult at first - away from everything and everyone but now things are much better.
>
> Anyway, things began to get better once we'd found somewhere to live. The company **put us up** in a hotel at first but we had to **look for** our own accommodation and that wasn't easy. Finally we were able to **take** someone else's flat **over** - they had suddenly decided to leave the company and the area for one reason or another. We **moved in** on Sunday. They brought all our stuff on Monday - boxes and boxes! - and we've been **sorting** them **out** ever since. We found one or two great shops nearby and have **picked up** some marvellous bits of furniture. We've now got a fantastic sofa-bed in the living-room so we can easily put friends up. (When are you coming?). The people round here are incredibly nice - we've already made lots of friends - people just seem to **pop in** all the time to chat and have a coffee. It's all very informal and I'm really enjoying that side of things.
>
> Jeff started his new job a couple of weeks ago. It's going very well, but he's working very long hours, I suppose that's inevitable at the beginning.
>
> All in all we're having a great time but we really miss you and hope you'll come out here soon. We'll probably be back for Christmas so we'll tell you more news then.
>
> Much love,
> Dee and Jeff.

Reading Task 2

Read the letter again and answer the following questions.

1 How long have the family been in San Francisco?
2 Where did they stay when they first arrived?
3 Where are they staying now?
4 What have they bought since they arrived?
5 What do they think of the Americans they have met so far?
6 When are they next going to see Jon and Trish?

Focus on Phrasal Verbs

Now, read the letter again and, *from the context*, try and decide the approximate meaning of each of the phrasal verbs.

settle in   ...... (*type 1*)   move in ...... (*type 1*)
put up   ...... (*type 2*)   sort out ...... (*type 2*)
look for   ...... (*type 3*)   pick up ...... (*type 2*)
take over ...... (*type 2*)   pop in   ...... (*type 1*)

Controlled Practice

A From the above list of phrasal verbs, put one in each sentence *in the correct form.*

1 If you could just .... me .... tonight, I promise I'll catch the first train home tomorrow morning.
2 You'll never guess who .... to my office the other day. It was Jim, Mike's old boss.
3 I hope Tony .... to his new school. It's the third time we've had to move him because of Simon changing jobs.
4 If you don't .... all those papers on your desk, I will!
5 I'm .... someone to do some secretarial work in the afternoons.
6 We've got a spare room. You can .... as soon as you like.
7 It's a great shop. If you've got time to look around you can .... some real bargains.
8 A really nice couple .... our flat when we left. We gave them our cats because we couldn't take them with us.

B Look at the following sentences and decide on the possible positions of the phrases/words in brackets.

Example:
I'll sort out in the morning (my room)
I'll sort out my room in the morning.
I'll sort my room out in the morning.

1 We put up for the night (him)
2 We put up for the night (Jon)
3 We settled in to our new home (quickly)
4 He picked up in that new shop (some interesting things)
5 He picked up in that new shop (them)
6 They looked for for their kitchen (some new chairs)
7 I will take over when he leaves (his flat)
8 I will take over when he leaves (it)
9 We are going to move in at the end of the month (to the house)
10 He popped in for a quick coffee (after the meeting)

Free Practice

Target language:
look for/move in/pick up/pop in/put up/settle in/sort out/take over

A   B

Look at these two pictures. Work in pairs. Study the information
given to you and then act out the conversation. Try to use the
phrasal verbs from this unit.

> **Student A.**
> Imagine that you have recently moved from the house in
> picture A to the house in picture B. Be prepared to tell
> someone about the experience.

> **Student B.**
> Your friend has recently moved from the house in picture A
> to the house in picture B. Ask her/him about the experience.
> You may want to ask about:
>
> - how s/he found the new house
> - why s/he moved
> - when s/he moved
> - the problems of moving
> - what needs to be done to the new house
> - the neighbours and the people in the village
> - the differences between living in the country and the city

Writing Task

Write to a friend describing your recent experience moving in to
the house in the picture above OR the house/flat you now live in.

12 Looking After

Child at school

Introductory Discussion Questions

'School – the happiest days of your life'

How do you feel about your school days?
Do/Did you enjoy your life at school? Why/Why not?

Listening Task 1

Read the questions then listen to the cassette.

1 Who is the conversation between?
2 What is the conversation about?

Listening Task 2

Listen again and answer these questions.

1 What does the teacher say positively about Brian?
2 What does the teacher say negatively about Brian?

Focus on Phrasal Verbs

A Listen to the dialogue again. Which of the following phrasal verbs do you hear in the text?

tell off   tell on   take off   take to   get up to   get down to
pick up   pick on   make out   make up   own up   take in
take up   look for   look after

B Now listen to nine extracts from the dialogue. Each one contains a phrasal verb. Write down exactly what you hear and then decide what the phrasal verb means in the context given.

1 .... (*type 2*)
2 .... (*type 2*)
3 .... (*type 4*)
4 .... (*type 4*)
5 .... (*type 3*)
6 .... (*type 2*)
7 .... (*type 1*)
8 .... (*type 1*)
9 .... (*type 3*)

Controlled Practice

A In pairs, ask and answer these questions.

1a) What takes up most of your time at the moment? Work/ a hobby/studying English . . .?
  b) Do you find it difficult to get down to doing English homework? How much time do you spend on it a day/a week?
2a) Were you 'good' when you were a child? Did you get up to anything particularly 'bad'?
  b) What reasons do children have for picking on other children? How can this be stopped?
  c) What would you do if your child stole sweets from a shop and was caught? Would you just tell them off?
3 In what circumstances might you make up a story that wasn't true?
4 If someone commits a crime and then owns up, what difference do you think that makes? Should the punishment be less? If so, why?
5 Can you take off any famous people?
6 Imagine that someone asked you to look after their dog for two weeks while they were on holiday. What information would you need?

B Four of these sentences are grammatically correct and four are not. Find the ones that are not correct and correct them. The first one has been done for you.

Example:
1 My teacher told off because I came to class late.
   NOT CORRECT.
   *My teacher told **me** off because I came to class late.*

2 He's very good at taking off politicians.
3 It is very quiet. I wonder what the children are getting up to now.
4 It is time to get to business down.
5 There were two older boys who always picked on me when I was at school.
6 Apparently, he make up the whole story.
7 She owned up to taking the money from his coat pocket.
8 He told me he wanted me to looking after his pet snake next week.

Free Practice

Target language:
get down to/get up to/look after/make up/own up/pick on/take off/take up/tell off

Work in pairs. Decide who is Student A and who is Student B. Prepare what you are going to say. Then act out the conversation. Use phrasal verbs from the unit where appropriate.

Student A.
You are Brian's teacher. Ask a colleague for advice. Explain the problem and then discuss what should be done.

Student B.
You are a teacher. Your colleague is having problems with a pupil called Brian. Listen to him describing the problems and then try and give some advice.

Writing Task

Brian has just been caught stealing cassettes from a music shop in the middle of town. You have been asked to write a report for the police and social worker about Brian's character/behaviour at school/home background. Make recommendations about what you believe should be done.

"I know the pet shop said he'd been well looked after but this is ridiculous."

13 *Giving Up*

Giving up smoking

"Kiss my lips."

"Kiss my ashtray."

Smoking. Who needs it?

Introductory Discussion Questions

1 Is the number of people who smoke increasing or decreasing in your country? Why do you think this is?
2 Do you think it is anti-social to smoke in public places? In which public places is it forbidden to smoke in your country? Do you think smoking should be prohibited in more or fewer places? Where?

Reading Task 1

Read the text quickly and decide where you think this text comes from.

Reading Text

HOW THEY GAVE UP

"I remember that ad on telly where the dad was in the garden and was always coughing and I suddenly thought you know if I *carry on* smoking, I could *end up* like that — not being able to do what I want. And that's when I gave up."
SALLY (10-15 a day for 5 years)

Only about one in three adults in Britain now smokes cigarettes.

Eleven million people in this country have *given up* smoking. Nine out of ten gave up on their own without any medical help. Some had to try several times before they gave up for good. Over half found it surprisingly easy.

This booklet is for all smokers who want to give up — young and old, heavy and light smokers. Whether you've tried before or not, you'll find some ideas that will help you to give up . . . for good.

"My wife and children *talked* me *into* giving up. We didn't have much money at the time and the price of cigarettes had just gone up again. The family was *going on* at me about all the things we could afford if I gave up. It was hard to stop but they all helped."
BRIAN (45 a day for 20 years)

" I tried to *cut down* but it didn't work. I had cut down and only smoked half as much as usual but then gradually it *crept up* again, so I decided I wouldn't smoke at all."
JULIE (30-40 cigarettes a day for 15 years)

"I tried three times. Finally I kept a packet on me so I had to *face up to* it. I used will power and nearly went mad for three weeks."
JOHN (20-40 a day for 6 years)

Reading Task 2

Read the text again and answer the following questions.

1 What is the aim of the booklet?
2 Who was the heaviest smoker?
3 What made Sally decide to stop?
4 Did John find it easy to stop?
5 Who helped Brian to stop?

Focus on Phrasal Verbs

Match the phrasal verbs in the text with the following meanings:

persuade   ...... (*type 3*)*
reduce   ...... (*type 2*)
confront   ...... (*type 4*)
finish   ...... (*type 1*)
stop   ...... (*type 2*)
increase slowly ...... (*type 1*)
continue   ...... (*type 3*)
say again and again ...... (*type 1*)

* This is different from normal type 3 phrasal verbs. There is usually an object *between* the verb and the preposition, and *after* the preposition.

Controlled Practice

1 Complete this conversation by putting in the phrasal verbs in their appropriate form.

Mike: Have you got a cigarette, Eddie?

Eddie: A cigarette? No, sorry. I've ...(a)... .

Mike: You're kidding!

Eddie: No, really, Mike. I ...(b)... completely last Tuesday.

Mike: Just stopped, just like that?

Eddie: Well, not exactly. I started ...(c)...in January. You know I was smoking about 30 a day last year. Well, Sophie was ...(d)...at me to stop. She said she couldn't stand the smell of cigarettes everywhere. So, finally, I had to ...(e)...the problem and I promised to stop – a little at a time. We agreed that I would smoke five a day less every month until I had ...(f)...completely.

Mike: That sounds like quite a good system.

Eddie: Have you thought about ...(g)...?

Mike: Of course. Who hasn't? With all the warnings about cancer and so on.

Eddie: Yeah, you don't want to ...(h)... like my brother-in-law.

Mike: Why? What's the matter with him?

Eddie: He's coughing all the time and he's always out of breath. It's terrible, but he just ...(i)...smoking 20 a day. He's mad! But, I think I was really convinced by the people at work. The number of non-smokers has been gradually ...(j)...and they have all been ...(k)...at me to stop. They have even complained that it is unfair of me to force them to breathe in polluted air, and I suppose they've got a point.

Mike: OK, OK you've ...(l)... me ...(l)... it. I'm convinced. I must stop, I know, but I need some help. I'm sure I'm going to find it very difficult.

2A Make appropriate questions for these answers using the
phrasal verb in brackets.

Example:
(give up)? Last year. I just don't have the time any more.
*When did you give up playing tennis? Last year. I just don't have
the time any more.*

1 (cut down)?   I don't need to. I don't drink that much!
2 (creep up)?   I don't know. Perhaps it's because of all the
                   advertising.
3 (carry on)?   I'm not sure. It depends if I get promotion soon
                   or not.
4 (end up)?   No, definitely not!
5 (face up to)?   I don't know. I never seem to have the time to
                   think about it.
6 (talk into)?   No, I think *you* should. He never listens to
                   anything I say.
7 (go on)?   He's just worried about you, that's all.

B Now make one different question to ask another student with
each of the above phrasal verbs.

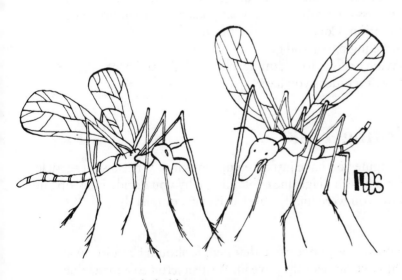

*"I feel old age creeping up on me –
it's nearly four-thirty . . ."*

Free Practice

Target language:
carry on/creep up/cut down/end up/face up to/give up/go on/talk into

---

1 Work in pairs. Decide who is Student A and Student B. Prepare what you are going to say. Then act out the conversation.

> **Student A.**
> Imagine you have a friend (Student B) who is a heavy smoker and wants to give up. Try and come up with as many different ideas to help her/him stop as possible.

> **Student B.**
> You are a heavy smoker and you want to give up. Speak to your friend (Student A) and ask for advice. Tell your friend what you have already done to try and give up.

2 Work in groups. Imagine you are part of a government campaign to cut down the numbers of young people who start smoking. Organise a plan of action.

OR

3 Work in groups of three or four. You are a group of friends who have become concerned about how little care the people in your school/workplace are showing towards the environment. Discuss the problem and what you can do to improve the situation. Consider possibilities for:
- recycling paper and glass
- saving energy, for example, electric light and heat
- any other ideas you have

Writing Task

1 Imagine you have just given up smoking. Write a short article for a health magazine explaining why you decided to stop and how you were finally able to give up completely.

OR

2 You are very concerned that people should be more aware of the environment they live in. Write a letter to a magazine explaining why you feel so strongly and what simple things people can do to improve the situation.

Setting Up

Borrowing money to open a restaurant

Introductory Discussion Question

What different services does a bank offer ordinary individuals?

Listening Task 1

Read the questions then listen to the cassette.

1 What does the customer, Mark Ellis, want?
2 Does he get it?

Listening Task 2

Now listen again and decide if the following statements are **true or false**.

1 Mark wants his first restaurant to be in the suburbs.
2 Mark has recently received £14,000.
3 Mark has found a possible building for his restaurant.
4 The building needs quite a lot of work doing to it.
5 The bank manager needs more information before he can make Mark a definite offer.

Focus on Phrasal Verbs

Listen to the conversation again and choose the correct meaning of each of these phrasal verbs:

1 fit in (*type 2*)   = find time to see/~~give an interview~~
2 set up (*type 2*)   = buy/start
3 come into (*type 3*)   = inherit/borrow
4 pick out (*type 2*)   = look for/choose
5 look over (*type 2*)   = examine/think about alternatives
6 do up (*type 2*)   = repair and decorate/buy furniture
7 branch out (*type 1*)   = expand/sell
8 fill in (*type 2*)   = look at/complete
9 turn down (*type 2*)   = refuse/consider

Controlled Practice

A Find the grammatical mistake in each sentence.

Example:
I'm terribly sorry, but I don't think we can fit in you *this week*.
I'm terribly sorry, but I don't think we can **fit you in** *this week*.

1 We're thinking of branching it out into men's clothes next year.
2 I can't believe it. She's come a fortune into.
3 Excuse me, madam, but have you picked it out the one you want yet?
4 He looked over on my article quickly and, without a word, threw it in the bin.
5 Of course, it needs do up, but basically it's a real bargain.
6 If you could just fill in, sir, with details of exactly what you saw and heard. Then you can go.
7 He's very upset. He never expected to be turn down.
8 We must to set up a committee to discover exactly what happened.

B i) Now, go back, look at each of the above sentences and decide what they are speaking about.
ii) Construct a short dialogue around each sentence demonstrating an appropriate context.

Example:
1 i) Expansion of range of stock.
  ii) A: *How's your business doing?*
      B: *Very well. As you know we have been concentrating on women's clothes and they have been so successful that* **we're thinking of branching out into men's clothes next year.**

A: *That's great, but does that mean you will have to look for new premises?*

B: *Probably later, but for the moment we're going to just have a new section in our existing shops.*

Free Practice

Target language:
branch out/come into/do up/fill in/fit in/look over/pick out/set up/turn down

---

A customer goes to his bank manager to try and get a loan. In roleplay 1, the customer wants to set up a business; in roleplay 2 the customer wants to buy a house. In pairs, choose a roleplay and then decide who is Student A and who is Student B. Study your role, then act out the conversation that takes place between them. Try to use the phrasal verbs from this unit.

1
> **Student A.**
> You are about to set up a small business. You need to borrow some money from the bank. Decide:
>
> - what business you want to set up
> - where you are going to set it up
> - how much money you want to borrow
> - plans for the future
>
> and any other information that you think might be important in the interview.

> **Student B.**
> You are a bank manager about to interview someone who wants to borrow some money to set up their own business. You must be very careful about who you lend money to, so prepare the different questions you are going to ask this customer. Be sure to ask about:
>
> - what type of business they want to set up
> - where they hope to set it up
> - what money they have to invest in the business
> - what experience/qualifications they have
> - what plans they have for the future
>
> and anything else that you think it is important to know.

OR

2 | **Student A.**
You are about to buy a house. You need to borrow some money from the bank. Decide

- what house you want to buy and what condition it is in
- where it is
- how much money you already have
- how much money you want to borrow and for how long
- how you will be able to repay the loan

Student B.
You are a bank manager about to interview someone who wants to borrow some money to buy a house. You must be very careful about who you lend money to, so prepare the different questions you are going to ask this customer. Be sure to ask

- what house it is and what condition it is in
- where it is
- how much money the buyer already has
- how much money the buyer wants to borrow and for how long
- how the buyer will be able to repay the money

You must be sure that the buyer will be able to repay the money on a regular basis and that the house is good security for the bank.

Writing Task

After the interview with the bank manager, Mark went home and told his wife what had happened. Write their dialogue.

Sticking Around

15

A private investigator in trouble

Introductory Discussion Question

Describe the stereotype of the typical American PI (private investigator). Consider character, clothes, lifestyle.

Reading Task 1

Read the text on the next page quickly to answer this question.

Who do you think the following people are and how are they connected?

a) I
b) Malone
c) the girl
d) Mike

Reading Text

I had been in more difficult spots — but not many. Malone had a gun pointed at my back; we were walking along the river, it was cold and it was dark. This case was *turning into* rather more than I expected. One thing was sure, I didn't want to **end up** like Eric — I turned cold at the memory of what his body had looked liked when they fished it out of the river.

We finally came to an old shed. Malone unlocked the door. Inside, sitting on a chair, was the girl I had been **looking for** since July. She was *tied up* and looked in bad shape. There were cuts on her face and legs. I could imagine what she had *been through*.

'Who are you? Don't I know you ...?' she said.

'It's the kind eyes and strong chin that *give* me *away*', I replied.

'Shut up', said Malone.

'Cigarette?' I offered.

He didn't answer.

We waited for something to happen ... then the phone rang.

'Yeah ... no ... yeah ... OK ... sure, boss'. Malone's responses were short and direct; a man of few words. Probably a great thinker.

He turned to me. 'Hey you. On the floor!'

'I think I'd prefer to stand, if that's OK', I replied politely.

It wasn't. 'On the floor or you die!' he shouted.

'OK, OK ... .' He could be quite persuasive at times.

As I was lying on the floor, Malone tied me up. He put a small packet in the corner of the room ... and then left. I heard him turn the key in the lock as he *went off*. I'd *come up against* some difficult situations in my time and this was another one to add to the list.

'What are we going to do now?' whispered the girl. She didn't seem totally confident in my ability to *get* us *out* of this situation. But then, neither was I. I tried to put on a brave face:

'*Stick around* kid, you ain't seen nothing yet.'

She still didn't seem very impressed. I wondered if Mike was going to *show up*, I'd left a message for him at the police station telling him where I was going, but then ... I suddenly realised that he was the only person I had told. So how had Malone found me so easily? I decided that I needed to talk to Mike sometime.

It was then I heard the ticking from the packet ... years of experience told me that Malone wasn't just concerned about us oversleeping.

269

Reading Task 2

Read the text again and then put the pictures in the correct order.

a)

b)

c)

d)

e)

f)

g)

h)

Focus on Phrasal Verbs

Say what you think each of the phrasal verbs means from their context in the above extract.

turn into	...... (*type 3*)
tie up	...... (*type 2*)
go through	...... (*type 3*)
give away	...... (*type 2*)
go off	...... (*type 1*)
come up against	...... (*type 4*)
get out	...... (*type 1*)
stick around	...... (*type 1*) [informal]
show up	...... (*type 1*)

Controlled Practice

A Match the halves of the dialogue.

Example: 1d)
Why don't you stick around a bit longer? I haven't really got time.

1 Why don't you stick around a bit longer?
2 Have you come up against this kind of problem before?
3 Do you think he'll show up?
4 Charles is turning into a little monster!
5 What was he tied up with?
6 I've never been through anything like it before.
7 How do you know he was angry?
8 How did you get out?
9 But will I recognise him?

a) I think it was some old pieces of rope.
b) I had to wait until the caretaker came with the key.
c) His height and strange clothes always give him away!
d) I haven't really got time.
e) Why? What happened exactly?
f) Well he just went off without saying a word.
g) Well, yes. In fact the same thing happened to me last year.
h) And he used to be such a lovely little boy!
i) Frankly no. He's so unreliable.

B Complete the following sentences with one of the phrasal verbs above in the correct form.

Example:
He *went off* without saying a word. I never saw him again.

1 I haven't often .... such a difficult individual.
2 Her accent .... her origins.
3 His work is gradually .... an obsession. He never does anything else.
4 Don't .... me ...., I promise I won't try to escape.
5 .... ! There's a bomb in the building!
6 I hope you don't have to .... an experience like that.
7 I don't know what I will do if he doesn't ....
8 What's the point of .... ? They aren't going to come now.

Free Practice

Target language:
come up against/get out/give away/go off/go through/show up/stick around/
tie up/turn into

Tell the story as if you were Malone. Look at the pictures in Reading Task 2 to help you remember what happened. Try and include the phrasal verbs in this unit.

Writing Task

Write a story about a different adventure this private investigator had. Try and include as many phrasal verbs from this unit as possible.

Revision Three
Cloze Text

Fill each gap with one word only. All the missing words come from phrasal verbs you have seen in the last five units.

Emma was not happy. It was time to leave London. Her parents, who were both English teachers, had decided to go to Spain to set ...(a)...a language school.

One day, at the beginning of July, the alarm clock ...(b)...off at 6am and they set off, with all their things, down to the south coast of Spain.

Some friends ...(c)...them up for the first couple of weeks while they looked ...(d)...somewhere to live and a possible building for the new school. In the end they decided to ...(e)...over a small, old hotel and do it ...(f)... . It was cheap and just what they wanted. They would use the first two floors for the school and the top floor as their flat. They moved ...(g)... immediately.

Emma started her new school the next day, but couldn't ...(h)...in. The other children already had their groups of friends and she was always alone. In fact some of them even ...(i)...on her and called her names because she spoke with a strong English accent.

Emma started coming home from school early. When her parents asked her why, she ...(j)...up stories about lessons being cancelled and teachers being absent. When they told her to get ...(k)...to her homework she would ...(l)...off to her room but just look out of the window wishing she was back home.

Sue and Richard had also come ...(m)..against problems with opening the school and the local bank had ...(n)...down their application for a loan. They decided they couldn't carry ...(o)...like this anymore. They would have to ...(p)...up to the fact that it wasn't going to work. It was time to go home.

Using a Phrasal Verbs Dictionary

A To help you in the future with other phrasal verbs that you
meet, you may want to use a phrasal verbs dictionary. Here are
some questions to help you understand the different
information a phrasal verbs dictionary can give you. All the
dictionary entries come from the Collins COBUILD Dictionary
of Phrasal Verbs (1989); the Longman Dictionary of Phrasal
Verbs, R Courtney (1983) and the Oxford Dictionary of
Current Idiomatic English (vol. 1 Phrasal Verbs, 1975). They
all refer to phrasal verbs that you have seen in the last five units.

1 *Collocation*

a) **own up**

> **own up.** If you **own up** to something wrong that you have done,
> you admit that you did it. EG *Come on, own up! Who did it? ... No-
> one owned up to taking the money.*
>
> V+ADV:
> ALSO+*to*

What word is *own up* often followed by?

b) **go on**

> **9** If someone **goes on** about something, or **goes on** at you, they
> continue talking to you about the same thing, often in an annoying
> way; an informal use. EG *I went on at my father to have safety belts
> fitted ... Don't go on about it ... Although his long book is funny,
> most of it is familiar, and it does go on.*
>
> V+ADV:
> ALSO+*about/at*

What two different words are *go on* (with this meaning) often
followed by?

2 *Deciding on Meaning*

a) **come into**

> **come into** *v prep* **1** to enter (a space such as a room or building): [IØ + *into*]
> *The door opened and the children came into the room. Come into the house and
> see my pictures. "Come into the garden, Maud."* (Alfred, Lord Tennyson, *Maud*)
> → **be in**[2] (1), etc.
> **2** to join (a group or activity): [T1 (*no pass.*)] *Several new members have come
> into the club since Christmas. We can run our own business without all the
> lawyers coming into it.*
> **3** to gain (something such as money) after someone's death: [T1 (*no pass.*, often
> simple tenses*)] *Charles came into a fortune when his father died* → **come in for** (2)
> **4** to begin to be in (a state or activity): [T1 (*no pass.*)] *High shoes came into fash-
> ion a few years ago. The trees should come into leaf soon. New companies come
> into existence every year. Your suggestions will come into consideration. New
> ways of thinking have come into being. The new machinery will come into use
> next week. You must have come into contact with someone suffering from an
> infectious disease. A new political party has come into power.* → **get into** (11), etc.

Which number meaning does *come into* have, as used in this sentence:

She came into a lot of money on her mother's death.

b)   **sort out**

sort out[1] [B1i pass adj] put, arrange, in groups, classes (according to size, shape etc). **S:** storekeeper, packer; teacher. **O:** part, fitting; box, tin; pupil, material □ *She spent a happy afternoon sorting out her coins and stamps.* □ *Members of the armed forces have been sorted out by trades and occupations.* MFM

sort out[2] [B1i pass] settle; order, set straight; straighten out[2] (q v). **O:** dispute, quarrel; matter, problem; tangle, muddle, confusion □ *You'd better send somebody over to sort the situation out.* □ *It's his job to sort out real grievances.* SC

sort out[3] [B1i pass] (informal) organize sb, make him behave in an orderly, disciplined way. **S:** leader, manager, teacher. **O:** force, unit; staff; class □ *'I'll give you a week to sort your men out, then I expect things to run smoothly.'* □ *I'll need time to sort out the office staff—they're hopelessly disorganized at the moment.*

sort out[4] [B1i pass] (informal) punish, chastize; handle, deal with[3] (q v), (in a fight). **S:** police, guard. **O:** trouble-maker, hooligan, bully □ *'If you don't stop that din, I'll come in and sort you out!'* □ *He went after the big fellow and really sorted him out.*

Which number meaning does *sort out* have, as used below:
*The room is in chaos. There are papers everywhere. I want you to **sort** them all **out** this morning.*

3   *Formal/Informal*

a)   **get up to**

get up to. When you talk about what someone **gets up to**, you are   V+ADV+PREP
referring to what they do, especially when it is something you do
not approve of; a very informal expression. EG *What did you get up
to while I was away?... When I found out what they used to get up to
I was absolutely horrified... I don't really think he'd get up to
anything behind my back.*

Who do you think would say this?:

*What did you
get up to while
I was away?*

i)   A parent to a child.
ii) A boss to an employee.

Why do you think this?

b)   **show up**

show up. 1 If you **show up**, you arrive at a place where people   V+ADV:
are expecting you; an informal use. EG *Over a hundred people*   USUALLY+A
*showed up at the meeting... How would his three new friends feel
about it if he showed up with his little brother?* ● **Turn up** means
almost the same as **show up**.

Which of these two sentences sounds strange? Why?

  i) *Mike **showed up** about half an hour late for the party.*
  ii) *The Queen **showed up** at 3.00pm to begin the ceremony.*

B To check that you can use the information in the dictionary effectively, try the following exercise. There is a dictionary entry about a phrasal verb you have seen in the last five units followed by two sentences which include the phrasal verb. One of the sentences is incorrect. Decide which sentence is incorrect and why. Think about *grammar* and *meaning*.

1   **talk into**

> **talk into.** If you **talk** someone **into** doing something, you per-   V+PRON+PREP,
> suade them to do it. EG *She talked me into taking a week's holiday...*   V+N+PREP,
> *He talked the Pondo leaders into ending the uprising... We can talk*   V+REFL+PREP
> *ourselves into anything.*

  a) He ***talked*** me ***into*** staying an extra hour.
  b) They were ***talked into*** sell the house for a very low price.

2   **pop in**

> **pop in.** If you **pop in**, you go to a friend's house or a shop casually.   V+ADV
> EG *They pop in for coffee and a chat... I can pop in tomorrow per-*
> *haps and let you know.*

  a) I am going to ***pop in*** for a job interview at the local bank this afternoon.
  b) I am home all day. Just ***pop in***, any time you like.

3   **end up**

> **end up** v adv 1 *not fml* to finish by becoming (something): [L1 (*as*) (*simple tenses*)] *In spite of the people's opinions, she ended up the winner. The general began his army life as a private soldier and ended up as ruler of his country.* [L7 (*simple tenses*)] *After gaining two fortunes, he ended up poor when he died.* →
> **fetch up** (4), **finish up** (2), **land up** (3), **wind up** (6).

  a) He should never have ***ended*** himself ***up*** like that.
  b) I don't want to ***end up*** without somewhere to live.

4   **branch out**

> **branch out** [A1] expand or develop in a new direction. **S:** factory, enterprise; he etc □ *Hitherto we have only been concerned with heavy metal castings; now we are **branching out** into light alloys and plastics.* □ *I see my Josephine is **branching out** on her own and breaking new ground.*

  a) He ***branched out*** and closed all the factories in the south.
  b) I want to ***branch out*** and perhaps start selling other types of electrical equipment.

5   tell off

tell off. If you **tell** someone **off**, you speak to them angrily because
they have done something wrong. EG *All the senior mistress does is
to tell the girls off for wearing the wrong colour blouse... He had a
reputation for telling off generals... If I was told off by my parents, I
could come along to the kitchen.* ● **Reprimand** is a formal word
for **tell off**.

V+PRON+ADV,
V+N+ADV,
V+ADV+N

a) I hate it when I get *told off* for something I didn't do!
b) I *told* the shop assistant *off* to the manager because he was
    so rude.

Student Competition: Phrasal Verb Dominoes

Materials required

● a table to play on
● verb and particle cards [see photocopiable sheet on p.74]

How to play

1   Divide the class into three teams.

2   One person in each team is the representative, who acts for the
    team.

3   Give each representative sixteen cards: eight verb cards and
    eight particle cards.

4   Put the remaining verb and particle cards in two piles on the
    table.

5   Representative A chooses and puts down one of her/his verb
    cards in the middle of the table [*put* in diagram 1]. This is the
    opening card. From now on cards can be put on the left or the
    right as in Dominoes.

6   Representative B now puts a particle card down which,
    together with the original verb card, should make a phrasal
    verb [*put off* in diagram 1]. Representative B should at the
    same time give a sentence including the phrasal verb correctly,
    for example, *The wedding was put off for another six months*.
    (The phrasal verb can be put in more or less any form, for
    example, active/passive, positive/negative/interrogative,
    past/present/future etc.) The phrasal verb and the example
    sentence can be judged correct or not by:

- consensus from the members of the other two teams
- reference to a (phrasal verbs) dictionary
- the teacher
- a combination of the above.

If it is decided the turn was not successful, the card that was placed should be taken back and the team should take an appropriate card from one of the two piles on the table. The turn then passes on to the next team ie in this case, Team C.

7 If Team B's response is judged to be satisfactory as above, then it is Team C's turn and they have the choice of either putting a particle to the left of *put* or a verb to the right of *off*. In our example they put *set* next to *off*.

8 A team can put down two cards at the same time if they know a verb + two particle combination. In diagram 1 you can see that Team A's second turn was *put **up with***.

9 If a team can't go they must pick up one card from one of the two extra piles and miss their turn.

10 The first team to put down all their cards calls 'Domino' and wins the hand. They receive the same number of points as there are cards left in the hands of the other teams.

11 If no team can play a card, the team with the least number of cards left wins.

Diagram 1

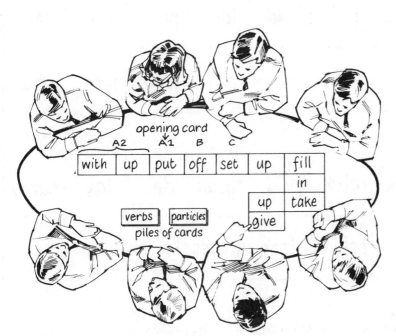

Phrasal Verb Dominoes

Team A

Verb Cards	call	fall	give	go	make	put	settle	talk
Particle Cards	up	out	off	in	on	down	back	with

Team B

Verb Cards	bring	cut	get	Keep	look	pull	show	take
Particle Cards	up	out	off	in	on	down	across	by

Team C

Verb Cards	break	come	fill	hold	let	pick	run	set
Particle Cards	up	out	off	in	on	down	into	through

Extra

Verb Cards	shut	work	catch	find	speak	do	lay	carry
Particle Cards	away	back	behind	after	across	through	over	into

© Richard Acklam 1992   This page may be photocopied for use in class.

Special Test Section

Complete these sentences with a phrasal verb that includes the verb in **bold italics**. Check that the phrasal verb is in the correct tense.

All the phrasal verbs are ones that you have seen in the book before.

Example:
Fill
Could you __fill__ this form __in__ before you leave?

Come
1 It's terrible. Pete's .... pneumonia. He is in hospital now.
2 I've .... quite a lot of money recently and I need to know how to invest it.
3 We've .... serious problems in finding the right person for the job.
4 He's .... a lot of criticism for what he said at yesterday's meeting.
5 If you .... my old school tie, can you let me have it?

Get
1 It's difficult to .... if you are unemployed. The money the government gives you just is not enough.
2 My father is always angry with me these days. It's really .... me .... .
3 How is it that so many people don't pay their taxes and .... it?
4 Do you .... Steve's parents?
5 I must .... to some work. I have to finish by 5pm.

Give
1 She .... all her possessions to charity and went to work with the poor in Calcutta.
2 He .... playing cricket at the weekends so that he could spend more time with his family.
3 His big smile .... how happy he was.
4 She .... all their books before starting the lesson.
5 She really wanted to go to the party. Finally her mother .... and said she could go.

Go
1 She .... working until she finished.
2 I'm sorry I'm late. My alarm clock didn't ....
3 My children have been .... at me to take them to the zoo.
4 If the price of petrol .... again, I will have to sell my car.
5 He has .... a lot in the last year: his wife left him, he lost his job and now his son is in prison.

Look

1 Could you .... my cats while I'm away on holiday.
2 When I see a word I don't understand I .... it .... in the dictionary.
3 We .... him all night, but we couldn't find him anywhere.
4 She .... me .... carefully from head to toe and then smiled with approval.
5 We're .... the problem of homelessness in our city.

Pick

1 I'll .... you .... from the station at about 8pm.
2 Will you help me .... some clothes for the party.
3 The other children .... him because he's quite fat. It's very cruel.
4 If things don't .... we may have to sell the business.
5 He .... his Italian by just talking to people in bars.

Put

1 We're going to .... his birthday party until the weekend when all his friends can come.
2 They were very kind. They .... me .... until I found a place of my own.
3 Why do you always .... me .... in front of other people? It's so embarrassing.
4 Could you .... me .... to the Customer Service Department, please?
5 How do you .... your boss? She's always so critical!

Take

1 He .... a year .... and travelled around South East Asia.
2 He .... his mother in the way he hates to be late for anything.
3 My doctor told me to .... a sport, so I would get more exercise.
4 I'm .... Brian's flat when he leaves. I'm moving in at the end of the month.
5 He said he was a policeman and I was completely ....

Reference Section

Remember...

Type 1 = verb + adverb (no object)
   Example: break down
         *The car **broke down** again last night and we had to walk.*

Type 2 = verb + adverb + object/verb + object + adverb
   Example: put off
         *We must **put off** the meeting for another week.*
         *We must **put** the meeting **off** for another week.*
         *We must **put** it **off** for another week.*
            But not
         *~~We must **put off** it for another week.~~*

Type 3 = verb + preposition + object
   Example: take after
         *He **takes after** his mother.*
         *He **takes after** her.*
            But not
         *~~He **takes** his mother **after**.~~*
         *~~He **takes** her **after**.~~*

Type 4 = verb + adverb + preposition + object
   Example: put up with
         *I can't **put up with** his behaviour any more.*
         *I can't **put up with** it any more.*

NB. If a phrasal verb *can* exist as a main verb and one particle, but is also often followed by a second particle, we categorise it as type 1 but indicate what the second particle is, for example **fall behind** (with something) [*type 1*].

The following list of phrasal verbs and their meanings includes all those to be found in this book. There are, of course, many more phrasal verbs and many of the phrasal verbs found below have more meanings than referred to here. For further information in this area you should consult a dictionary of phrasal verbs, for example, the Collins COBUILD Dictionary of Phrasal Verbs (1989).

BLOW [something] **UP**   (type 2):   **destroy by an explosion**   Unit 10
    Example: *The commandos blew up the bridge and then attacked the base.*

Unit

BRANCH OUT (type 1): **expand/do something** new 14
Example: *Business is going well. We are thinking of branching out into children's clothing as well as adults'.*

BREAK DOWN (type 1): **stop working** 8
Example: *The car has broken down again. That's the third time this month.*

BREAK INTO [something] (type 3): **enter illegally** 10
Example: *The thieves broke into our house while we were on holiday.*

BRING [something] **DOWN** (type 2): **reduce** 3
Example: *We must bring the price of the tickets down if we are going to be competitive.*

BRING [someone] **UP** (type 2): **to raise/educate children** 9
Example: *I wouldn't like to bring a child up as a single parent.*

CALL [someone] **BACK** (type 2): **return a phonecall (no passive)** 2
Example: *Could you call Mr Jones back this afternoon?*

CALL [something] **OFF** (type 2): **cancel** 2
Example: *You can't call the wedding off now. Everything has been arranged.*

CARRY ON (type 3): **continue** 13
Example: *He carried on working after everyone else had gone home.*

CARRY [something] **OUT** (type 2): **do** 6
Example: *The nurses carried out all their duties quickly and efficiently.*

CATCH ON (type 1): **understand** 1
Example: *He catches on very quickly. You never have to explain twice.*

CLEAR [something] **UP** (type 2): **to organise/make tidy** 10
Example: *We must clear up the spare room before your mother comes to stay.*

COME ACROSS [something] (type 3): **find unexpectedly** 10
Example: *I came across a photo of my grandmother yesterday when I was cleaning the attic.*

COME DOWN WITH [an illness] (type 4): **contract illness** 6
Example: *Most of the people in my office have come down with flu. I think I am going to be next!*

Unit

COME IN FOR [something]   (type 4):   **receive criticism or**   3
blame
    Example: _He has come in for a lot of criticism for the way_
           he treated his wife.

COME INTO [money/property]   (type 3):   **inherit**   14
    Example: _He's come into a fortune. It's incredible. I_
           didn't realise his father was so rich.

COME OUT IN [something]   (type 4):   **show the signs of**   6
an illness
    Example: _John's not very well. He's come out in little red_
           spots all over his body and he's got a high
           temperature.

COME UP AGAINST [something]   (type 4):   **face**   15
difficulty
    Example: _We've come up against one or two problems in_
           trying to get support for the idea.

COUNT ON [someone/something]   (type 3):   **depend on**   2
    Example: _I am counting on you to show me what to do._

CRACK DOWN [on someone/something]   (type 1):   **take**   3
strong action against
    Example: _The government is going to crack down on_
           football hooligans.

CREEP UP   (type 1):   **increase slowly**   13
    Example: _The inflation rate has crept up during the last_
           year.

CUT BACK [on something]   (type 1):   **reduce something**   5
because you can't afford it
    Example: _The government has cut back on public_
           spending.

CUT [something] **DOWN**   (type 2):   **reduce the**   13
size/amount
    Example: _He cut down the number of hours he was at_
           work from 60 to 55 a week.

CUT [something] **OFF**   (type 2):   **when a service, for**   7
example, gas/telephone is disconnected (often passive)
    Example: _The gas was cut off last week because we forgot_
           to pay the bill.

DO AWAY WITH [something]   (type 4):   **destroy/abolish**   3
    Example: _We are going to do away with the old tax_
           system.

Unit

DO [something] **UP**   (type 2):   **repair/decorate a building**   14
Example: *The house doesn't look very nice now but when we've done it up it will be fantastic.*

END UP   (type 1):   **finish in a certain situation**   13
Example: *If we continue like this we shall end up with no money at all.*

FACE UP TO [something]   (type 4):   **confront, accept and deal with something unpleasant**   13
Example: *You must face up to the fact that you are probably going to lose your job.*

FALL BEHIND [with something]   (type 1):   **fail to do something by a certain date**   7
Example: *If you fall behind with your payments again, we will take back the car.*

FALL THROUGH   (type 1):   **when an arrangement fails to take place**   5
Example: *We were going to buy that house, but it fell through because the bank wouldn't lend us the money.*

FILL [something] **IN**   (type 2):   **complete (a form)**   14
Example: *He has filled in the job application form.*

FILL [something] **UP**   (type 2):   **make full**   8
Example: *Could you fill up this jug with water for the flowers, please?*

FIND [something] **OUT**   (type 2):   **discover**   1
Example: *He found out that the course didn't start for another week.*

FIT [someone/something] **IN**   (type 2):   **find time for**   14
Example: *Can you fit me in tomorrow afternoon, doctor?*

GET [something] **ACROSS**   (type 2):   **communicate**   1
Example: *I don't know if I got my message across.*

GET AWAY WITH [something]   (type 4):   **escape criticism/punishment**   3
Example: *That's the third time you have been late this week. You are not going to get away with it again.*

GET BY   (type 1):   **have just enough**   1
Example: *We haven't got much money but we get by.*

GET [someone] **DOWN**   (type 2*):   **depress (no passive)**   7
Example: *I hate this weather. It's really getting me down.*

*The object never goes after the particle *down*.

	Unit

GET DOWN TO [something]　(type 4):　**start doing** 　12
something/seriously
    Example: _It is time to get down to business._

GET ON [with someone]　(type 1):　**have a good** 　4
relationship with someone
    Example: _I get on very well with my youngest brother._

GET OUT [of something]　(type 1):　**escape** 　15
    Example: _We were locked in the room. There was no way_
           to get out.

GET OVER [something]　(type 3):　**recover from** 　4
something, get better
    Example: _It took him more than two years to get over the_
           death of his mother.

GET ROUND [something]　(type 3):　**avoid** 　5
    Example: _He tried to get round the problem by asking_
           them to change the rules in this case.

GET THROUGH [to someone]　(type 1):　**make contact** 　2
(by phone)
    Example: _I've been trying to get through to you all_
           afternoon but the line is always busy!

GET UP TO [something]　(type 4):　**do something naughty** 　12
or bad
    Example: _It's very quiet. What do you think the children_
           are getting up to now?

GIVE [something] **AWAY**　a)　(type 2):　**distribute for free** 　7
    Example: _He gave away all his books to friends, before he_
           left.

GIVE [something] **AWAY**　b)　(type 2):　**reveal** 　15
    Example: _His accent gave away the fact that he originally_
           came from Scotland.

GIVE IN　(type 1):　**surrender/agree to demands** 　4
    Example: _It doesn't matter what you say, he will never_
           give in.

GIVE [something] **OUT**　(type 2):　**distribute** 　10
    Example: _He gave out information about the new training_
           courses to everyone at the meeting.

GIVE [something] **UP**　(type 2):　**stop** 　13
    Example: _He gave up playing football at the weekends_
           because he didn't have enough time.

GO OFF　a)　(type 1):　**explode (especially a bomb)** 　10
    Example: _A bomb went off but no one was hurt._

Unit

GO OFF b) (type 1): **leave**   15
   Example: *He went off without saying a word.*

GO ON a) (type 1): **happen**   4
   Example: *Something strange was going on and I wanted
            to know what it was.*

GO ON b) (type 1): **continue**   7
   Example: *He went on fighting even after I told him to
            stop.*

GO ON [at someone] **c)** (type 1): **say repeatedly**   13
   Example: *I have been going on at my mother to have new
            locks put in.*

GO OUT [with someone] (type 1): **have a romantic or**   4
sexual relationship
   Example: *My sister has been going out with Tom for three
            months. I think it is quite serious.*

GO UP (type 1): **increase**   3
   Example: *The price of sugar will go up 5% at the end of
            this month.*

GO THROUGH [something] (type 3): **experience**   15
something
   Example: *We had to wait at the airport for 36 hours. I
            never want to go through that again.*

GROW UP (type 1): **to change from being a child to being**   9
an adult
   Example: *This is the town where I grew up.*

HOLD ON (type 1): **wait**   2
   Example: *Could you hold on for five minutes please?*

HOLD [someone/something] **UP** (type 2): **delay**   8
   Example: *I was held up in the traffic for nearly two hours.*

KEEP ON (type 1): **continue**   9
   Example: *They kept on looking for the little girl until it
            got too dark.*

KEEP UP [with someone/something] (type 1): **maintain**   1
the same level as
   Example: *She walks so fast, I can never keep up with her.*

LAY [someone] **OFF** (type 2): **stop employing people due**   5
to external factors
   Example: *Our company has laid off another 100 people
            this week.*

	Unit

LAY [someone] **UP** (type 2): **cause to stay in bed,** **generally through accident or illness (often passive)** — 6
> Example: *He was laid up for three weeks after the car accident.*

LET [someone] **DOWN** (type 2): **not do what you say you will do** — 2
> Example: *He has let me down again. I specifically asked him to meet me here at 8.00pm at the latest and he is not here.*

LET [someone] **OFF** (type 2): **give no punishment, or very small punishment** — 3
> Example: *He was let off with a warning.*

LET [someone] **OUT** (type 2): **release** — 10
> Example: *They let him out of prison after only ten years, because of his good behaviour.*

LIVE UP TO [something] (type 4): **be as good as expected** — 9
> Example: *She certainly didn't live up to Mike's description of her.*

LOOK AFTER [something/someone] (type 3): **take care of** — 12
> Example: *She looked after her father for several years before he died.*

LOOK FOR [something/someone] (type 3): **try to find** — 11
> Example: *I looked for my keys all morning but I couldn't find them.*

LOOK INTO [something] (type 3): **investigate** — 3
> Example: *The police are looking into the strange circumstances of Mr Jenkin's death.*

LOOK [someone/something] **OVER** (type 2): **examine the condition of** — 14
> Example: *We are going to look the house over next week. It sounds as if it is just what we want.*

LOOK [something] **UP** (type 2): **check in reference material** — 1
> Example: *I don't like reading English newspapers because there are too many words that I need to look up.*

LOOK UP TO [someone] (type 4): **admire and respect** — 9
> Example: *He's always looked up to his older brother. Personally, I don't understand why. He seems so ordinary.*

Unit

MAKE OUT (type 1): **pretend**   4

    Example: *He made out that he was a friend of Pete's but I*
             knew it wasn't true. Pete would have told me.

MAKE [something] **UP** **a)** (type 2): **replace what is**   8
missing, regain

    Example: *He made up the hours he had missed by*
             working all night.

MAKE [something] **UP** **b)** (type 2): **invent**   12

    Example: *You know all those things he said about*
             fighting in the war. Well, he made it all up.
             None of it was true.

MOVE IN (type 1): **start living in a new place**   11

    Example: *We are going to move in on Friday. You must*
             come and see us.

OWN UP [to something] (type 1): **admit**   12

    Example: *He owned up to breaking the window with the*
             football.

PASS OUT (type 1): **lose consciousness**   6

    Example: *She passed out while she was waiting to see the*
             doctor.

PICK ON [someone] (type 3): **treat badly, unfairly**   12

    Example: *It's awful. The bigger boys at school are always*
             picking on him.

PICK [something] **OUT** (type 2): **choose**   14

    Example: *We went shopping this morning and managed*
             to pick out some very nice clothes.

PICK [something] **UP** **a)** (type 2): **learn**   1

    Example: *It's incredible how quickly he picked up*
             Chinese.

PICK UP **b)** (type 1): **increase/improve**   5

    Example: *Don't worry. Business is definitely picking up.*

PICK [someone/something] **UP** **c)** (type 2): **take**   8
someone in your car

    Example: *My dad is going to pick me up from the party at*
             midnight.

PICK [something] **UP** **d)** (type 2): **buy unexpectedly**   11

    Example: *We picked up some real bargains in the summer*
             sales.

Unit

POP IN   (type 1):   **visit, probably without warning**   11
(informal)
    Example: *I think I'll pop in on my mother and see how*
            she is as I am going past her house anyway.

PULL [something] **OFF**   (type 2):   **achieve something**   10
difficult
    Example: *The magician pulled off an amazing trick.*

PULL OUT [of something]   (type 1):   **withdraw**   5
    Example: *He pulled out of the competition due to back*
            injuries.

PULL THROUGH   (type 1):   **survive**   6
    Example: *It was a very serious accident but I think he is*
            going to pull through.

PULL UP   (type 1):   **vehicle slows down and stops**   8
    Example: *Did you know that a large black car has just*
            pulled up outside your front door?

PUT [someone] **AWAY**   (type 2):   **send to prison**   3
    Example: *He was put away for five years for the bank*
            robbery.

PUT [something] **BY**   (type 2):   **save**   7
    Example: *We try to put £50 a month by for emergencies.*

PUT [someone] **DOWN**   a)   (type 2):   **make someone feel**   9
inferior
    Example: *He seems to like putting women down. It's*
            terrible.

PUT [an animal] **DOWN**   b)   (type 2):   **kill**   10
    Example: *Toby, our dog, was very old and in constant*
            pain. So, we asked the vet to put him down.

PUT [something] **OFF**   (type 2):   **postpone**   2
    Example: *We put the match off for a week because of the*
            rain.

PUT [someone] **THROUGH**   (type 2):   **connect**   2
    Example: *I am putting you through to Ms Phillips now.*

PUT [someone] **UP**   (type 2):   **give accommodation**   11
    Example: *I can put you up for the rest of this week. I've*
            got a spare room.

PUT UP WITH [something, someone]   (type 4):   **tolerate**   4
    Example: *I don't think I can put up with him any more.*
            He's so rude all the time.

RIP [someone] **OFF**   (type 2):   **cheat financially (informal)**   7
    Example: *I paid £100 for the watch. I think I was ripped off.*

RULE [something] **OUT**   (type 2):   **decide something isn't**   3
possible
    Example: *You mustn't rule out the idea of leaving the job.*

RUN OUT [of something]   (type 1):   **have no more left**   8
    Example: *We have run out of sugar. Could you go and buy some more?*

RUN [someone/something] **OVER**   (type 2):   **hit with a**   8
vehicle
    Example: *This little girl crossed the road without looking. I nearly ran her over but fortunately I managed to stop just in time.*

SET OFF   (type 1):   **start on a journey**   8
    Example: *We decided to set off very early so that we would arrive before it got dark.*

SET [something] **UP**   (type 2):   **start a company, committee**   14
etc
    Example: *We want to expand our business. We are thinking of setting up offices in France, Spain and Italy.*

SETTLE IN   (type 1):   **become comfortable in a new**   11
situation
    Example: *It didn't take long for her to settle into her new job.*

SETTLE UP   (type 1):   **pay back money owed**   7
    Example: *I promise I will settle up as soon as my father sends me some more money.*

SHOOT UP   (type 1):   **increase dramatically**   5
    Example: *Our rent shot up last month. We are now paying twice as much as this time last year!*

SHOW OFF   (type 1):   **try to impress people by making**   9
certain qualities/achievements very obvious
    Example: *I hate him! He's always showing off about how much money he's got.*

SHOW UP   (type 1):   **arrive**   15
    Example: *I don't think he will show up now. It's nearly midnight.*

	Unit

SHUT UP (type 1): **stop talking (informal)**   1
Example: *She doesn't really want conversation. She just wants you to shut up and listen.*

SORT [something] OUT (type 2): **put in order**   11
Example: *I want to spend the weekend sorting out my study. At the moment it is in chaos.*

SPEAK UP (type 1): **speak louder**   2
Example: *You must speak up a little, I can't hear very well.*

SPLIT UP (type 1): **when a relationship finishes and the couple separate**   4
Example: *Mike and Julie split up last summer but I think they want to get back together again now.*

STICK AROUND (type 1): **stay, wait (informal)**   15
Example: *I am going to stick around until he comes.*

TAKE AFTER [someone] (type 3): **be similar in appearance/character to older relative**   9
Example: *He's very good-looking. He takes after his father.*

TAKE [someone] IN (type 2): **deceive**   4
Example: *He was very nice to me all evening but I wasn't taken in. I knew that he just wanted to borrow some more money.*

TAKE OFF a) (type 1): **begin to increase dramatically**   5
Example: *Sales of the new European newspaper have taken off to the surprise of many critics.*

TAKE [time] OFF b) (type 2): **spend time doing something different from your usual work**   6
Example: *We took two months off in the summer and travelled around South East Asia.*

TAKE [someone] OFF c) (type 2): **imitate to make people laugh**   12
Example: *He's very good at taking off the headmaster.*

TAKE [something] OVER a) (type 2): **gain control of**   5
Example: *ABC Ltd has been taken over by a large American corporation and most of the senior management has been replaced.*

Unit

TAKE [something] **OVER** b) (type 2): **occupy property** 11
    Example: *I am taking over his flat from the end of*
        August when he moves back to England.

TAKE [something] **UP** a) (type 2): **start a new activity** 9
    Example: *I am going to take up tennis this summer.*

TAKE UP b) (type 1): **occupy (time/space etc.)** 12
    Example: *Playing cricket takes up the whole of every*
        weekend so I will have to stop.

TALK [someone] **INTO** [something] (type 3*): **persuade** 13
    Example: *It didn't take me long to talk her into*
        working an extra day.

        *This is different from normal type 3 phrasal verbs. There is
        usually an object *between* the verb and the preposition, and
        after the preposition.

TELL [someone] **OFF** (type 2): **speak to someone** 12
critically because they have done something wrong
(especially adults to children)
    Example: *The teacher told him off for being rude.*

TIE [someone/something] **UP** (type 2): **fasten with** 15
rope/chain
    Example: *He tied her up and left her in the dark with*
        nothing to eat or drink.

TURN [someone/something] **DOWN** (type 2): **refuse** 14
    Example: *He turned the job down even though the*
        salary was very good.

TURN INTO [something] (type 3): **become** 15
    Example: *She has turned into a very unpleasant person.*

WEAR [someone] **OUT** (type 2): **to make tired/exhaust** 6
    Example: *The children wear me out. After a day with*
        them I just want to go to bed and sleep.

WORK [something] **OUT** (type 2): **calculate, decide** 1
    Example: *He couldn't work out why she had become*
        so angry.

Tapescripts

Unit 2
Getting Through
Listening Text

Operator: Hello. Britex Ltd. Can I help you?

John Stevens: Yes. I'd like to speak to Karen Miller in Marketing.

Operator: *Putting* you *through*.

Operator: I'm sorry but the line's busy at the moment. Can you *hold on*?

John Stevens: Yes. That's fine.

Operator: You're through now, caller.

Karen Miller: Hello?

John Stevens: Hello Karen. This is John Stevens from Comtec.

Karen Miller: Who? Sorry, this isn't a very good line. Could you *speak up* please?

John Stevens: Yes, sorry. This is John Stevens from Comtec.

Karen Miller: Oh, hello John. What can I do for you?

John Stevens: Well, actually, I'm phoning about next week's meeting.

Karen Miller: You mean the one on Thursday?

John Stevens: Yes, that's right. Thursday the 24th at 9.30am.

Karen Miller: You don't want to *call* it *off*, do you?

John Stevens: No, not at all. But we need to *put* it *off* for at least a week.

Karen Miller: Oh, why's that?

John Stevens: Well. We're having problems getting all the figures together.

Karen Miller: I see. Have you told Jack Ryan?

John Stevens: No, not yet. I haven't been able to *get through* to him. I've left a message but he hasn't *called* me *back* yet.

Karen Miller: Fine. When were you thinking of?

John Stevens: To be on the safe side, why don't we say the 5th or the 6th of November.

Karen Miller: Just a minute. I need to check my diary. In fact I think the 5th would be better for me. Same time?

John Stevens: Yes, that's fine.

Karen Miller: And you're sure you're going to be ready by then? This meeting is extremely important for us. You know that we are *counting on* you.

John Stevens: Yes, absolutely. No question. We've never *let* you *down* before, have we?

Karen Miller: No, true. Good. Well, see you on the 5th then.

John Stevens: OK. Thanks very much. Bye.

Karen Miller: Bye.

Focus on Phrasal Verbs

1 *Putting* you *through*
2 Can you *hold on*?
3 Could you *speak up* please?
4 You don't want to *call* it *off*, do you?
5 We need to *put* it *off* for at least a week.
6 I haven't been able to *get through* to him.
7 He hasn't *called* me *back* yet.
8 You know that we are *counting on* you.
9 We've never *let* you *down* before, have we?

Unit 4
Getting On
Listening Text

C: Have you seen Julie lately? Do you know how she is?

L: ... Oh Julie? Well, actually, not very well at all. It's that husband of hers!

C: Why? What's happened now?

L: Well ... you know they got married a year ago?

C: Yeah, they didn't know each other very well, did they?

L: No. They'd only been *going out* for six months before that, but they seemed to *get on* really well together. Anyway, recently, a friend of Julie's saw Mike, the husband, in a restaurant, with a very attractive young woman. They seemed to be more than just good friends!

C: Oh no! Poor Julie! What did she do?

L: Well, she asked Mike to explain exactly what was *going on*.

C: What did he say?

L: He tried to *make out* that the woman was a business client and, at first, Julie was *taken in*.

C: So, what happened?

L: Well, he seemed to be having a lot of 'business dinners' in the evenings.

C: Yeah, it's a familiar story ...

L: ... and on one or two occasions she even smelt perfume on his clothes which wasn't hers ...

C: How awful for her!

L: Then, one day, she found this letter.

C: What do you mean? What kind of letter?

L: A love letter ... all very predictable.

C: Who was it from?

L: There was no name ... just the words 'I love you' and the letter 'P' at the end.

C: Did she know who it was?

L: She had an idea but, anyway, she told Mike she knew what was **going on** and she couldn't *put up with* it any more. She confronted Mike with all the different things she'd noticed and insisted he told her the truth.

C: So what did he do then?

L: At first he again tried to **make out** that nothing was the matter, but finally, after she refused to believe him, he admitted he was in a terrible state, that he didn't know what to do. He said he felt he loved Julie but he'd also fallen in love with Patricia (the other woman). Julie's first reaction was to tell him to leave at once ... that she never wanted to see him again.

C: And did she?

L: Well no ... you see, apparently, at that point, he begged her to let him stay and promised never to see Patricia again. Finally, she *gave in* and so, they're still together.

C: When did all this happen?

L: Oh, about a month ago.

C: Has she *got over* it yet?

L: No, not really. I don't know if she ever will. I wouldn't be surprised if they *split up* in the end. She's really unhappy ...

Revision One
Mistake Search

On Friday morning at 8.00am Brian Hawkins went to work as usual. He walked to the underground station, waited a few minutes for his train on the crowded platform, and then got on. As usual he had to **put up with** standing the whole way.

At Victoria, where a large number of passengers always change, Brian felt someone push past him aggressively. It was a tall, well-dressed young man. At first Brian couldn't **work out** what was happening and then he felt for his wallet. To his horror, he realised it wasn't there and it had all his credit cards plus over £100 in cash. Brian couldn't believe that he had been **taken in** by such an old trick. He was furious. He certainly wasn't going to let this guy **get away with** it that easily.

He tried to **find out** where the young man had gone. Finally he saw him on the platform. He ran out of the train, grabbed the man and pulled him back towards the train. The man tried to **make out** that he didn't know what was **going on**.

Brian jumped back into the train just as the doors were closing. The doors shut on the young man's coat,

trapping him. A look of panic crossed his face as the train started to move. The train slowly accelerated and the young man had to run to **keep up** with the train. Just as the train was leaving the station and the young man was about to come off the end of the platform, he pulled himself away from the train and fell backwards onto the platform.

That evening, when Brian got back home, he was just about to tell his wife the whole story, when she asked him how he'd managed to **get by** without any money.

'What do you mean?' Brian asked.

'Well, you left your wallet here on the kitchen table when you went to work this morning.'

Unit 6
Pulling Through
Listening Text

Doctor: Good morning, Mrs Barrett. How's your mother feeling?

Patient: Much better thank you.

Doctor: I told you you didn't need to worry. I said she'd *pull through* even though it was a bad fall.

Patient: The only problem is she doesn't like the idea of being *laid up* for such a long time. Two months in bed seems endless to her.

Doctor: I know. It's very unfortunate. And what about you? How can I help you?

Patient: Well, doctor, it's only a small thing and I'm probably wasting your time but a few weeks ago I *came out in* this rash ... see, here on my left arm.

Doctor: Mmm yes ... not very nice.

Patient: Well, normally I wouldn't have come and bothered you about it but yesterday afternoon I felt really awful and ... you see ...

Doctor: Yes ...

Patient: I was just picking up a box of books when suddenly I felt very strange and then apparently I *passed out* because the next thing I knew, Judy, my daughter, was standing over me helping me drink some water. I had a funny taste in my mouth and at first I thought I was going to be sick but I wasn't. I did have to go and lie down on my bed for the rest of the afternoon though.

Doctor: You're the fourth person I've seen today who seems to have *come down with* the same thing. It looks like a virus is going around. How have you been feeling in general recently?

Patient: Well, it's funny you should ask, only I never

have any energy. I seem to be *worn out* all the time. I get tired so quickly, and we have such a lot to do at the office at the moment.

Doctor: You have a job?

Patient: Yes, a part-time job doing translation for a local firm.

Doctor: Look, I really think you should *take* a few days *off*. Also I want you to take some extra vitamins and a tonic ... Let me just write you the prescription ... There, now, if it isn't better within a couple of weeks come back as we may have to *carry out* a blood test. But don't worry, most people seem to get better very quickly.

Unit 8
Breaking Down
Listening Text

Mary: Steve ... John ... at last! Come in ... give me your coats. So ... you finally got here!

Steve: Yes. We're so sorry. We really did *set off* early as planned.

Mary: Well, what happened then? Why are you so late?

Steve: Basically, a series of disasters. First of all, I'd agreed to *pick* John *up* on the way and he wasn't ready of course!

Mary: Typical!

John: Hey, that's not fair. That wasn't the only thing that made us late. In case you'd forgotten, we *ran out* of petrol, just outside Lincoln. Now that certainly wasn't my fault.

Steve: OK, OK ... as it happens I forgot to *fill up* last night. In fact I went to the garage especially to get petrol but when I got home I realised I'd bought my cigarettes but no petrol. Well, we all make mistakes!

John: Yes, you certainly do. It was really embarrassing. We were in this really narrow country road. There was nowhere to *pull up* out of the way of the traffic, so we just had to stop in the middle of the road! We *held up* all the other traffic for well over half an hour.

Steve: Yes, well, I really did try and *make up* the lost time after that. I didn't want to be late. I mean it's not every day you're twenty-one.

Mary: So, was the rest of the journey OK?

John: Not at all. That was just the beginning! The next thing that happened was when we were going through this small village ...

Steve: Oh yes ... do you mean when that child ran out into the road in front of us?

John: That's right ... I was sure you were going to *run* her *over*.

Steve: Me too. How I managed to stop in time I will never know.

Mary: Goodness me. How awful! Was she all right?

Steve: Oh yes, *she* was fine. But you can imagine the kind of state I was in.

Mary: Yes. You must have felt terrible.

John: And that's not all!

Mary: Oh no, there surely isn't more?

Steve: Would you believe it, but we were almost here when the car *broke down*.

John: What do you mean 'almost here', we've been walking for the last half an hour in the pouring rain!

Mary: Well, don't just stand there ... come and have a drink. You look like you both need one!

John: You can say that again. Is there any birthday cake left?

Mary: Yes I think so, but you'll have to be quick!

Focus on Phrasal Verbs

1 We really did *set off* early as planned.
2 I'd agreed to *pick* John *up* on the way.
3 we *ran out* of petrol
4 I forgot to *fill up* last night.
5 There was nowhere to *pull up*
6 We *held up* all the other traffic.
7 I really did try and *make up* the lost time.
8 I was sure you were going to *run* her *over*.
9 we were almost here when the car *broke down*.

Unit 10
Blowing Up
Listening Text

Good evening. This is Mark Sullivan on the 9 o'clock news.

The main story tonight – a bomb has *gone off* in the centre of Birmingham today. The explosion happened around 4pm. Nobody was hurt, but windows were broken in nearby shops. No-one has claimed responsibility for placing the bomb. Here in London, army experts *blew up* a small brown package that had apparently been left outside a well-known store. Members of an animal rights group *broke into* experimental laboratories in Sussex late last night and *let out* large numbers of the animals being kept there. A spokesperson for the group said that the animals were in a terrible state. They were being used to test new cosmetic products on. Most of the animals are now being cared for by members of the group, although some have had to be *put down*.

Members of Greenpeace today were out in force around Westminster, *giving out* leaflets protesting against the destruction of the tropical rainforests in South America.

And now – sport. The FA Cup final between Manchester United and Liverpool has had to be postponed due to bad weather conditions. The new date has been set as the 28th of this month. Liverpool are hoping to *pull off* a double victory, having just come top of the First Division for this season.

And finally, Mr J Arkwright of Duck Pond Road, Hackney has had some good news today. It has been confirmed that he is the owner of three genuine drawings by Picasso. He said to reporters earlier today that he just *came across* them while he was *clearing up* his attic. The sketches have been valued at approximately £250,000.

And that's it from me. Have a very good evening.

Unit 12
Looking After
Listening Text

Teacher: Hello . . . you must be Mr Jenkins, Brian's Dad.

Mr Jenkins: That's right. And you are Mrs Edmonds?

Teacher: Yes, that's right. I'm so glad you could come this evening. You see, I've been wanting to have a word with you about Brian . . .

Mr Jenkins: There's nothing wrong, is there? He's not having problems with his schoolwork, is he?

Teacher: Oh no. Brian's a very bright young boy, he learns fast – the only trouble is . . .

Mr Jenkins: . . . He can be a bit too much at times. Don't I know! I hope you *tell* him *off* when he needs it.

Teacher: Yes, well, quite. You see, in class Brian tends to be quite noisy and he's very good at *taking off* some of the members of staff.

Mr Jenkins: Oh, he's just the same at home. He's always *getting up to* something.

Teacher: That's not so bad, but he seems to find it difficult to *get down to* his work and he can't concentrate for long.

Mr Jenkins: I see.

Teacher: Does Brian **get on** with his younger sister?

Mr Jenkins: Yes. I think so. Of course, they fight

sometimes, that's normal isn't it?

Teacher: I only ask because I understand Brian's been *picking on* some of the smaller boys in the class – nothing very serious, but just making life difficult for them. And then last week he apparently took some money from the coat of another boy.

Mr Jenkins: No! I really don't believe that. You must be mistaken. I always give him plenty of money.

Teacher: Well, I asked him directly about it. At first he *made up* a story about the boy having given him the money but finally he *owned up* that he had taken it.

Mr Jenkins: I see. Look . . . I don't know how much you know about all this but Brian's mother has been in hospital. It's been hard trying to take care of Brian and his sister on my own, and do my job at the same time. In fact, just recently, work has been *taking up* a lot of my time. I haven't really had much time for Brian to be honest. I've been getting home at 8 or 9 o'clock. I just have time to get Brian and Rachel some supper and then they go to bed. It's awful – I never seem to see them.

Teacher: Who *looks after* them when you're not there?

Mr Jenkins: There is a woman who comes in.

Teacher: Yes. I can see that it hasn't been easy.

Mr Jenkins: So, what do you think I ought to do?

Focus on Phrasal Verbs

1 I hope you *tell* him *off* when he needs it.
2 he's very good at *taking off* some of the members of staff.
3 He's always *getting up to* something.
4 he finds it difficult to *get down to* his work
5 Brian's been *picking on* some of the smaller boys
6 At first he *made up* a story
7 finally he *owned up* that he had taken it.
8 work has been *taking up* a lot of my time.
9 Who *looks after* them when you're not there?

Unit 14

Setting Up
Listening Text

Bank Manager: Come in, come in. Please sit down.

Mark: Thank you. Thanks very much for *fitting* me *in*. I know you must be very busy.

Bank Manager: Not at all. We do try to be available as much as possible.

Mark: Well, as you know, I've come to see if there is any chance of the bank lending me some money to help me *set up* a small restaurant in the centre of town.

Bank Manager: Yes, well . . . I need to ask you one or two questions to start with.

Mark: Of course.

Bank Manager: Do you have any capital of your own?

Mark: Well, in fact, I've just *come into* some money. You see my grandmother recently died and left me £40,000 which I wanted to use for the business.

Bank Manager: I see. And have you actually *picked out* a suitable location, a building for the restaurant?

Mark: Yes, I think so. In Lincoln Road. It's on the ground floor. It used to be a small supermarket but it went bankrupt. I've *looked* it *over* quite carefully. It's not in very good condition and we need to *do* it *up* a bit but that means it will be much cheaper to buy.

Bank Manager: Fine. And how about future plans?

Mark: Well obviously I will see how things go at first but really I'd like to *branch out* after a year or two and open up in the suburbs if things go well.

Bank Manager: Right, well, you just need to *fill in* this form with a few details and send it to us as soon as you can. Then we can arrange a meeting to discuss terms.

Mark: So you don't think I'm going to be *turned down*?

Bank Manager: I really can't say at this stage. We need to see all the relevant information first and then we'll be in a better position to . . .

Key

The Grammar of Phrasal Verbs

a) correct
b) correct
c) correct
d) not correct He went along with her idea to grow vegetables in the garden.
e) not correct Are you going to give it back?
f) not correct The plane took off three hours late.
g) correct
h) not correct He got in the bus and sat down.
i) correct

Unit 1 Introductory Discussion Questions

Here are some ways of learning English which apply to other languages. There are other ways too.

- go to a language class
- work from language teaching books/cassettes at home/in the car
- read newspapers/magazines/books in English
- listen to the radio in English (for example, BBC World Service)
- visit English-speaking countries etc.

Reading Task 1

1 The text is an extract from a letter.
2 A young person who has recently arrived in the Middle East or North Africa to work there.
3 A friend or relation. Someone the writer knows well.

Reading Task 2

1
- goes to language classes and does homework
- has conversations with local people
- looks up new words in the dictionary and learns them by heart

2 Yes, reasonably. *As for my Arabic ... well, things are not going too badly ...*
*All in all, I feel I'm able to **get by** in Arabic for the day-to-day things*

Focus on Phrasal Verbs

communicate – get across
survive – get by
discover – find out
keep quiet – shut up
learn – pick up

understand – catch on
maintain the same level – keep up
look for information in a reference book – look up
mentally calculate – work out

Controlled Practice

A

1 His father told him to shut up.
2 Look it up if you don't know what it means./
   If you don't know what it means look it up.
3 It was difficult to get the idea across./
   It was difficult to get across the idea.

4 I've got enough Spanish to get by on holiday.
5 I can't work out what he means.
6 They could not catch on to what I was saying.
7 I picked up the job by watching the other workers./
I picked the job up by watching the other workers.
8 He walks so fast that I can't keep up with him.

B

Here are some ways of beginning and finishing the sentences. There are many other ways possible.

1 I sometimes find it difficult to keep up *when he speaks very quickly.*
2 I catch on quickly when *the teacher gives lots of clear examples.*
3 I can't work out why *he is so unfriendly.*
4 *If you speak the teacher always corrects your mistakes* and so I shut up!
5 *It was a new word for me* and so I looked it up in a dictionary.
6 *I was unemployed for six months and life was hard* but I managed to get by.
7 *I spent a long time explaining my idea* but I couldn't get across what I meant.
8 *I really enjoyed learning Italian* and I picked it up very quickly.

Unit 2 Introductory Discussion Questions

1 Here are some reasons why people find speaking on the telephone in a foreign language difficult but there are other reasons too.

- no visual contact
- need to speak and respond quickly
- need for certain set phrases etc

2 There are many set phrases used particularly on the telephone. Here are some useful ones:

- Could I speak to Sarah Green please?
- Could you put me through to the Sales Department please?
- Hello. John Brown speaking.
- Could you hold on please?
- Can I call you back later? etc.

Listening Task 1

1 He wants to speak to Karen Miller to change the date of next week's meeting.
2 Yes.

Listening Task 2

John Stevens, who works for **Comtec**, phoned **Karen Miller**, who works for **Britex Ltd**. He wanted to change the date of their meeting originally arranged for **Thursday 24th at 9.30am** because of **problems getting all the figures together**. They agreed a new date of **5th November at 9.30am** but John still has to contact **Jack Ryan**.

Focus on Phrasal Verbs

A/B

return the call – call back
wait – hold on
postpone – put off
connect – put through
cancel – call off

make contact – get through
fail/disappoint – let down
depend on – count on
talk louder – speak up

C

1 **Putting** you **through**. *(type 2)*
2 *Can you **hold on**? (type 1)*
3 *Could you **speak up** please? (type 1)*
4 *You don't want to **call** it **off**, do you? (type 2)*
5 *We need to **put** it **off** for at least a week. (type 2)*
6 *I haven't been able to **get through** to him. (type 1)*
7 *He hasn't **called** me **back** yet. (type 2)*
8 *You know that we are **counting on** you. (type 3)*
9 *We've never **let** you **down** before, have we? (type 2)*

Controlled Practice

A

2 not correct   Please hold on. Mr Jameson will be with you in a minute.
3 not correct   Don't let me down. I really need your help this time.
4 correct
5 correct
6 not correct   Please call me back before this evening.
7 correct
8 correct
9 not correct   Is your phone broken? I can never seem to get through to you.
10 correct
11 not correct   Please speak up. I can't hear you.
12 correct

Unit 3   Introductory Discussion Questions

2 Here are some explanations for violence at football matches: Other
  explanations are possible too.
  • deliberate troublemakers who start fights, who are not interested in football
  • supporters drink before the match and become aggressive
  • boring lives and other sources of frustration, for example, having no job etc
    are expressed through violence at football matches

Reading Task 1

1 It is a letter to a newspaper.
2 To express support for the presence of police at football matches.

Reading Task 2

1 Clubs will be stopped from playing in other countries.
2 Stricter punishments for offenders.

Focus on Phrasal Verbs

go up – increase
bring down – reduce
crack down – take strong action against
get away with – escape criticism/punishment
come in for – receive
look into – investigate
rule out – decide something isn't possible
put away – send to prison
let off – give no punishment or very small punishment
do away with – abolish

Controlled Practice

A

1c/2e/3g/4a/5h/6d/7f/8b

B

1 do away with	6 rule out
2 look into	7 crack down
3 going up	8 get away with
4 put away	9 bring down
5 let (you) off	

Unit 4 Introductory Discussion Question

There are many reasons why people end relationships. Here are some. They may

- be unhappy
- be bored
- meet someone else
- have grown apart from their partner etc.

Listening Task 1

1 Julie and Mike.
2 Mike has been seeing another woman (Patricia).
3 No.

Listening Task 2

1 True. one year and six months
2 False. four things:
- Mike seen in restaurant with attractive young woman
- lots of 'business dinners'
- perfume on his clothes
- love letter

3 True.
4 False. _Julie's first reaction was to tell him to leave at once . . ._
5 True.

Focus on Phrasal Verbs

have a (romantic) relationship – go out
have a good relationship with someone – get on
happen – go on
pretend – make out
deceive – take in
tolerate – put up with
agree to someone else's demands – give in
recover from – get over
finish a relationship and separate – split up

Controlled Practice

1 a) going out   f) gave in
   b) taken in   g) got over
   c) going on   h) getting on
   d) made out   i) split up
   e) put up with

2 **Julie and Mike**

Got married one year ago.

Were going out for six months before that.

When Julie found out the complete truth she didn't put up with it and didn't leave but she told Mike to leave.

They haven't got over it yet.

The narrator thinks that they *will* split up in the end.

Amanda and Kevin

Got married five years ago.

Were going out for two years before that.

Amanda put up with it at first but then said she was going to leave.

They have got over it.

The narrator doesn't think that they will split up in the end.

Unit 5 Introductory Discussion Question

1 Here are some factors which affect the success of companies. There are, of course, others.

- the economic situation in the country
- demand for their product
- level of efficiency/productivity within the company etc.

Reading Task 1

1 No.
2 Yes, in general.

Reading Task 2

1 Hitec is not doing well because the cost of raw materials has shot up during the last year.
  Electrix is doing well because of the development of some exciting new models.
2 It is going to cut back on its Manchester workforce. It has pulled out of the American market.
3 It has difficulties keeping up with production requirements. It has lost a deal with Formatco due to failure to agree on certain key issues of design.

Focus on Phrasal Verbs

1 shoot up   = increase a lot   6 take over   = take control of
2 cut back   = reduce   7 pick up   = get better
3 lay off   = sack   8 take off   = begin to increase rapidly
4 pull out   = withdraw from   9 fall through   = not happen
5 get round   = avoid

Controlled Practice

A

1 He was pulled out of the competition at the last minute by his trainer because of problems with his leg.
2 not possible in the passive
3 not possible in the passive
4 A number of administrative staff are going to be laid off as a result of a massive reorganisation programme.
5 The number of nurses can't be cut back (on)!
6 not possible in the passive
7 This problem must be got round. Perhaps we could ask your father's advice.
8 not possible in the passive

B

picking up

C

These are some possible responses. There are many others.

1 They shot up by 50%.
2 I was laid off on Friday.
3 No, he's pulled out because he is still having problems with his leg.
4 No, there are ways of getting round him.
5 I'm sure it will take over one or two small European companies.
6 It's picked up since I met this girl called Cindy at a party a few weeks ago.
7 Sales of our newest product have taken off. It's amazing!
8 No, that's all fallen through. We couldn't agree on a price.

Revision One Mistake Search

A

b), a), f), e), d), c).

B

put up from – put up with
work up – work out
taken off – taken in
get away by – get away with
find up – find out

make off – make out
going through – going on
keep down – keep up
get down – get by

Phrasal Verb Square

A

let down/put off/look up/lay off/keep up/speak up/pick up/shut up/split up

B

1 let (you) down
2 shut up
3 pick up
4 lay off
5 split up

6 speak up
7 put off
8 look up
9 keep up

Unit 6 Introductory Discussion Questions

2 Here are some characteristics of a good doctor. There are many others.
- sympathetic
- patient
- knows latest techniques
- explains carefully
- up-to-date medical knowledge

Listening Task 1

1 She goes to see the doctor because she has a rash and has been feeling strange recently.
2 She recommends that Mrs Barrett doesn't go to work for a few days and takes some extra vitamins and a tonic.

Listening Task 2

1 She had a bad fall.
2 She's got a rash on it.
3 Her daughter, Judy.
4 Three.
5 She works as a part-time translator.

Focus on Phrasal Verbs

A

pull through – be all right, survive.

lay up – cause to stay in bed (as a result of accident/illness)

come out in – show the signs of illness

pass out – lose consciousness

come down with – catch (a virus/disease)

wear out – make very tired

take (time) off – spend time doing something different from your usual work

carry out – do

B

a) Mrs Barret's mother is in a hospital bed after a serious fall, but she is going to **pull through** all right. However, she will be **laid up** in bed at home for a while.

b) Mrs Barrett's arm has **come out in** a rash.

c) Mrs Barrett **passed out**. She is sitting on the floor and her daughter is helping her to drink a glass of water.

d) Other people have **come down with** the same thing just recently.

e) Mrs Barrett has been **worn out** a lot of the time recently.

f) The doctor thinks that Mrs Barrett should **take** a few days **off**.

Controlled Practice

A

Here are some situations and dialogues showing how and when the sentences might be said. Many other answers are possible however.

1 Possible situation: someone talking about an accident they had in the past.
   Possible dialogue:
   – *Have you ever had a really bad accident?*
   – *Yes. I was once driving a motorbike down the motorway when a car drove in front of me with no warning. I fell off and was hit by another car. **And, do you know, I was laid up for six months!***

2 Possible situation: parent talking about family illnesses.
   Possible dialogue:
   – *So, how was your holiday?*
   – *Not very good I'm afraid. The hotel wasn't very clean, the food was rather strange **and all the children came out in these strange red spots.***
   – *So, what did you do?*

3 Possible situation: someone talking about an incident at a party.
   Possible dialogue:
   – *Did you enjoy the party last night?*
   – *Yes, but did you hear what happened?*
   – *No, tell me.*
   – *John fainted half way through the evening. **One minute he was standing there, the next he had passed out.** It was really alarming.*
   – *How awful. Was he all right?*

4 Possible situation: someone doing a street survey and stopping passers-by.
   Possible dialogue:
   – ***Excuse me, sir. We are carrying out a survey on attitudes to the national health system.***
   – *I am very sorry but I don't have time.*
   – *It won't take a minute, sir.*
   – *Sorry.*

5 Possible situation: someone with flu, talking to a friend.
   Possible dialogue:
   – *How are you? You don't look very well.*
   – *I'm not. I've got flu.*
   – *Have you? So has everyone in my family except me.*
   – **I hope you don't come down with it as well.**
   – *So do I!*

6 Possible situation: someone being asked to go and play tennis with friends.
   Possible dialogue:
   – *Claire, can you come and play tennis with us?*
   – **I can't. I'm absolutely worn out.** *I've been lifting boxes for my dad all morning.*

7 Possible situation: one secretary asking another if she thinks the boss will give her some days holiday.
   Possible dialogue:
   – **Do you think he'll let me take a few days off?**
   – *I don't know. We are very busy at the moment.*
   – *But I haven't had any holiday for months.*

B

1 He's rather tired now. The children wore him out with all their questions.
2 First, he came out in spots, and then he became very hot and feverish.
3 I'm not surprised he passed out after drinking all that beer.
4 I took two weeks off in July.
5 We all came down with flu over Christmas.
6 If I don't pull through, will you take care of the children?
7 He's like a dictator. I am apparently just here to carry out his orders.

Unit 7   Reading Task 1

Not really. It gave them different kinds of problems.

Reading Task 2

1 Arthur lost his job and couldn't get another. Consequently they didn't have enough money to pay their mortgage or telephone bill. Arthur began drinking.
2 They lost most of the money and most of their friends.

Focus on Phrasal Verbs

save – put by	distribute – give away
continue – go on	depress – get down
cheat – rip off	disconnect – cut off
be late – fall behind	pay back – settle up

Controlled Practice

A

1d/2g/3f/4a/5h/6b/7e/8c

B

1 go on	5 give away
2 ripped off	6 fell behind
3 getting (him) down	7 put (a little money) by
4 settle up	

Unit 8 Listening Task 1

b)

Listening Task 2

- John wasn't ready to leave at the time arranged
- they ran out of petrol
- they nearly ran over a child
- the car broke down and they had to walk the rest of the way

Focus on Phrasal Verbs

1 We really did *set off* early as planned.
  set off – leave
2 I'd agreed to *pick* John *up* on the way.
  pick up – stop for and take (in a vehicle).
3 we *ran out* of petrol
  run out – have no more left
4 I forgot to *fill up* last night.
  fill up – make full (with petrol in this case)
5 There was nowhere to *pull up*.
  pull up – slow down and stop
6 We *held up* all the other traffic.
  hold up – delay
7 I really did try and *make up* the lost time.
  make up – get back/regain
8 I was sure you were going to *run* her *over*.
  run over – hit
9 we were almost here when the car *broke down*
  break down – stop going/working

Controlled Practice

A

1 I will pick you up from/at the station at 8.30pm tomorrow evening.
2 He filled up the car before they went on the journey yesterday.
3 John, we have run out of milk again! That is the third time this week.
4 Look! A large black car has pulled up/is pulling up in front of our house.
5 We were held up for several hours at the airport because of a bomb scare.
6 He promised to make up the lost time by working in/through his holidays.
7 I have never actually run anybody over but I did once hit a cyclist.
8 If the/my car breaks down again I will/am going to sell it!

B

These are possible sentences. There are many others.

1 I was held up in a traffic jam.
2 No. I am going to fill it up right now.
3 My mum's picking me up.
4 I hope I can make up the time by taking the motorway.
5 A police car has pulled up outside our house.
6 Well, we set off very early.
7 I once nearly ran someone over because they weren't looking.
8 No, I'm sorry, we have run out.

Unit 9 Introductory Discussion Questions

There are many reasons why problems exist between children and parents. Here are some:

- children and parents have different political/moral values
- children want to do something with their lives that their parents don't approve of (for example leave school early)
- children have friends parents don't like etc.

Reading Task 1

Sarah is John's girlfriend/wife. Maureen is John's mother.

Reading Task 2

John wants his father to be proud of him, but his father is disappointed in John's decision to become a dancer.

Focus on Phrasal Verbs

take after – be similar in appearance/character to older relative
look up to – admire, respect
put down – make someone feel inferior
grow up – change from being a child into becoming an adult
show off – try to impress people by making certain qualities/achievements very
        obvious
bring up – raise/educate children
keep on – continue
live up to – be as good as expected
take up – start a new activity

Controlled Practice

A *Someone/Something?*

look up to someone
put someone down/put down someone
grow up
show off
bring someone up/bring up someone
keep on
live up to something
take something up/take up something

B

1 She says he takes after his father.
   She says he takes after him.
2 I am going to take up golf.
   I am going to take golf up.
   I am going to take it up.
3 She always shows off in front of new people.
   She always shows off in front of them.
        NB. You could say
        She always shows them off in front of new people
        but that refers to a different meaning of **show off**.
4 I remember Julie when she was growing up.
   I remember her when she was growing up.
5 If he keeps on playing that music I am going to get angry.
   If he keeps on playing it I am going to get angry.
6 It wasn't easy to bring up a young son on my own.
   It wasn't easy to bring a young son up on my own.
   It wasn't easy to bring him up on my own.
7 Do you think he will live up to his reputation?
   Do you think he will live up to it?
8 He looked up to his sister because she was so clever.
   He looked up to her because she was so clever.

Unit 10 Listening Task 1

1 Five
2 • bomb explosion in Birmingham
   • animal rights group broke into laboratories
   • Greenpeace distributing leaflets
   • FA Cup final
   • discovery of Picasso sketches

Listening Task 2

1 False. Nobody was hurt.
2 True.
3 False. They were distributing leaflets about the destruction of the tropical
   rainforests.
4 False. The match has been postponed.
5 True.

Focus on Phrasal Verbs

enter illegally – break into
destroy with an explosive device – blow up
kill – put down
find by chance – come across
distribute – give out
put in order – clear up
achieve – pull off
explode – go off
free – let out

Controlled Practice

A

1 The terrorists blew *it* up last night.
2 complete
3 They broke into *it* as soon as it was dark.
4 You must let *it* out! It's cruel to keep an animal in such a small space.
5 The vet said *it* should be put down.
6 complete
7 It's incredible – they've pulled *it* off again.
8 I came across *it* this morning. It was behind my desk.

B Here are some things which *it* could refer to. There are other possibilities.

1 a car/a building etc.
3 a building/a safe
4 an animal
5 an animal
7 a victory/a bank robbery
8 an object, for example, a pen/a mouse

C These are possible sentences. There are others.

1 It was blown up by a bomb.
2 Someone broke into the safe.
3 I decided to let them out.
4 Yes. We might have to put him down.
5 They are giving out information about the dangers of nuclear power.
6 I think if everything goes well he could just pull it off.
7 Actually, I came across it the other day at the back of my desk drawer.
8 I'm clearing up the guest bedroom before my father arrives on Sunday afternoon.

Revision Two Multiple choice

1b) 2d) 3c) 4b) 5a) 6a) 7d) 8c) 9c) 10a)

Phrasal Verbs Crossword

Unit 11 Introductory Discussion Question

These are some of the things you have to do when you move house. There are others.

- find the new accommodation
- arrange to move all your things
- tell people of your change of address
- arrange for the services (gas, electricity, telephone) to be connected

Reading Task 1

1 They are basically positive.
2 Two reasons are mentioned:
- the local people are very friendly
- Jeff's job is going well
  They conclude by saying *All in all we're having a great time.*

Reading Task 2

1 Two months (beginning of August to 3rd October 91 [date on letter]).
2 In a hotel.
3 In a flat which was previously occupied by someone who worked for the same company.
4 Some furniture including a sofa-bed.
5 They like them very much.
6 At Christmas.

Focus on Phrasal Verbs

settle in – become comfortable in a new situation
put up – give accommodation
look for – try to find
take over – occupy property
move in – start living in a new place
sort out – put in order
pick up – buy unexpectedly
pop in – visit, probably without warning

Controlled Practice

A

1 put (me) up
2 popped in
3 settles in
4 sort out
5 looking for
6 move in
7 pick up
8 took over

B

1 We put him up for the night.
2 We put up Jon for the night.
  We put Jon up for the night.
3 We settled in quickly to our new home.
  We settled in to our new home quickly.
  We quickly settled in to our new home.

4 He picked up some interesting things in that new shop.
   He picked some interesting things up in that new shop.
5 He picked them up in that new shop.
6 They looked for some new chairs for their kitchen.
7 I will take over his flat when he leaves.
   I will take his flat over when he leaves.
8 I will take it over when he leaves.
9 We are going to move in to the house at the end of the month.
10 He popped in after the meeting for a quick coffee.
   After the meeting he popped in for a quick coffee.
   He popped in for a quick coffee after the meeting.

Unit 12   Listening Task 1

1 A parent, Mr Jenkins, and schoolteacher, Mrs Edmonds.
2 The parent's young son, Brian.

Listening Task 2

1 *Brian's a very bright young boy, he learns fast . . .*
2 *Brian tends to be quite noisy/he finds it difficult to get down to his work . . . he can't concentrate for long/ Brian's been picking on some of the smaller boys in the class . . . he apparently took some money from the coat of another boy/At first he made up some story . . .*

Focus on Phrasal Verbs

A

tell off/take off/get up to/get down to/pick on/make up/own up/take up/
look after

B

1 *I hope you **tell** him **off** when he needs it.*
   tell off – speak to someone critically because they have done something wrong
2 *. . . he's very good at **taking off** some of the members of staff.*
   take off – imitate to make people laugh
3 *He's always **getting up to** something.*
   get up to – do something naughty or bad
4 *he finds it difficult to **get down to** his work.*
   get down to – start doing seriously
5 *Brian's been **picking on** some of the smaller boys*
   pick on – treat badly, unfairly
6 *At first he **made up** a story*
   make up – invent
7 *finally he **owned up** that he had taken it.*
   own up – admit
8 *work has been **taking up** a lot of my time.*
   take up – occupy
9 *Who **looks after** them when you're not there?*
   look after – take care of

Controlled Practice

B

2 correct

3 correct

4 not correct It is time to get down to business.

5 correct

6 not correct Apparently, he made up the whole story.

7 correct

8 not correct He told me he wanted me to look after his pet snake next week.

Unit 13 Reading Task 1

A booklet giving advice on how to stop smoking.

Reading Task 2

1 To help people stop smoking.

2 Brian.

3 A television advertisement.

4 No.

5 His family.

Focus on Phrasal Verbs

persuade – talk into

reduce – cut down

confront – face up to

finish – end up

stop – give up

increase slowly – creep up

continue – carry on

say again and again – go on

Controlled Practice

1

a) given up

b) gave up

c) cutting down

d) going on

e) face up to

f) given up

g) giving up

h) end up

i) carries on

j) creeping up

k) going on

l) talked (me) into

2A

These are some possible questions. There are many others.

1 Are you going to cut down how much whisky you drink?
2 Why do you think sales of cigarettes are creeping up?
3 Are you going to carry on working here?
4 Do you want to end up like Mr Jones?
5 When are you going to face up to this problem?
6 Are you going to try and talk him into staying?
7 Why does he always go on at me about working harder?

Unit 14 Introductory Discussion Question

These are some of the services offered by banks.
- current accounts
- deposit accounts
- overdrafts
- loans
- financial advice
- foreign exchange etc.

Listening Task 1

1 He wants a loan from the bank.
2 Not immediately, he must give the bank manager more information before a decision can be made.

Listening Task 2

1 False. He wants it to be in the centre of town.
2 False. Mark has recently received £40,000.
3 True.
4 True.
5 True.

Focus on Phrasal Verbs

1 fit in   = find time to see
2 set up   = start
3 come into   = inherit
4 pick out   = choose
5 look over   = examine
6 do up   = repair and decorate
7 branch out   = expand
8 fill in   = complete
9 turn down   = refuse

Controlled Practice

A

1 We're thinking of branching out into men's clothes next year.
2 I can't believe it. She's come into a fortune.
3 Excuse me, madam, but have you picked out the one you want yet?
4 He looked over my article quickly and, without a word, threw it in the bin.
5 Of course, it needs doing up, but basically it's a real bargain.
6 If you could just fill it in, sir, with details of exactly what you saw and heard. Then you can go.
7 He's very upset. He never expected to be turned down.
8 We must set up a committee to discover exactly what happened.

Bi)

2 Someone they know who has inherited a large amount of money.
3 Enquiring if the customer has chosen what she wants.
4 Reaction of tutor/boss to what they have written.
5 The house/boat or whatever they are trying to sell.
6 An official form, possibly requiring details of the crime/accident witnessed.
7 Someone they know who didn't get the job they had applied for/a place at university.
8 Organising a committee to find the cause of what happened (possibly an accident).

ii) Here are some examples of possible dialogues:

2
A: *Do you know Julie at work?*
B: *Who? You mean, Julie in accounts.*
A: *Yes, that's right. Well, **I can't believe it. She's come into a fortune**.*
B: *No! Really! How?*
A: *An old aunt died and left her half a million pounds.*

3
A: *Can I help you madam?*
B: *Yes, I'm looking for an elegant black evening dress.*
A: *They are over there at the back.*
B: *Thank you.*
[a little later]
A: ***Excuse me, madam, but have you picked out the one you want yet?***

4
A: *So, did you get your story on the front page?*
B: *Well, you know I had been preparing it for days and I knew it should be the front page story. My one problem was that the editor hated me. At 6pm on Monday night I walked into his office nervously and handed him what I had written. Do you know what he did?*
A: *No.*
B: ***He looked over my article quickly and, without a word, threw it in the bin.***

5
A: *Isn't this a wonderful house? Lots of character.*
B: *Yes, but ...*
A: *Beautiful garden out the back and only ten minutes walk from the station.*
B: *Yes, but there are holes in the roof, there's no paint on the walls ...*
A: ***Of course, it needs doing up, but basically it's a real bargain.***

6

A: *Why did you bring me here Officer?*

B: *As you saw the accident we would like you to tell us everything you know.*

A: *Well, what do you want me to do with this form?*

B: ***If you could just fill it in, sir, with details of exactly what you saw and heard.
Then you can go.***

7

A: *What's the matter with John. He looks terrible. Is it because he didn't get that
job?*

B: *Yes. **He's very upset. He never expected to be turned down.***

A: *I think everyone was very surprised.*

8

A: *Everyone is very angry about what happened. We want to know why all that
water was polluted.*

B: *You're absolutely right. **We must set up a committee to discover exactly what
happened.***

Unit 15 Introductory Discussion Question

Clothes: often not well-dressed, typically wears a plain raincoat in all weathers,
possibly a trilby hat

Lifestyle: irregular, often works at night. Eats fast food. Generally looks
exhausted. Office is in chaos and shabby, obviously doesn't make much money
from the business.

Character: Looks slow and not very clever, but in fact very aware of what is going
on and constantly assimilating new information, clues etc. Will often take on
cases for free to help deserving causes.

Reading Task 1

1a) **I:** the private investigator.

 b) **Malone:** the bad guy, probably carrying out orders for The Boss.

 c) **the girl:** the victim, possibly kidnapped by Malone for some reason.

 d) **Mike:** probably a policeman (the message was left at the police station) who
 is a friend of the private investigator.

It looks like the private investigator has been hired to find the girl and has been
captured by Malone. This is possibly because Mike has informed Malone of the
private investigator's plans.

Reading Task 2

c), e), h), a), d), g), f), b).

Focus on Phrasal Verbs

turn into – become
tie up – fasten with rope/chain
go through – experience
give away – reveal
go off – leave
come up against – face difficulty
get out – escape
stick around – stay, wait (informal)
show up – arrive

Controlled Practice

A

1d/2g/3i/4h/5a/6e/7f/8b/9c

B

1 come up against
2 gave away/gives away
3 turning into
4 tie (me) up

5 get out
6 go through
7 show up
8 sticking around

Revision Three Cloze Text

a) up
b) went
c) put
d) for
e) take
f) up

g) in
h) settle
i) picked
j) made
k) down
l) go

m) up
n) turned
o) on
p) face

Using a Phrasal Verbs Dictionary

A 1 _Collocation_

a) **own up** is often followed by **to**.
b) **go on** is often followed by **at** or **about**.

2 _Deciding on Meaning_

a) **come into** has meaning number 3.
b) **sort out** has meaning number 1.

3 *Formal/Informal*

a) i) A parent would say this to a child because ***get up to*** is generally used in informal contexts.

b) ii) The second sentence sounds strange because ***show up*** is also generally used informally.

B

1b) is incorrect. ***Talked into*** needs to be followed by a verb+ing. The correct sentence would be:

They were talked into <u>selling</u> the house for a very low price.

2a) is incorrect. ***Pop in*** is an informal expression which indicates a <u>casual</u> arrangement, not a formal/official one as in this example.

3a) is incorrect. The two parts of the phrasal verb ***end up*** cannot be separated.

4a) is incorrect. ***Branch out*** means to extend your activities, not to reduce them.

5b) is incorrect. You can ***tell*** someone ***off*** for (doing) something, but you cannot ***tell*** someone ***off*** <u>to someone else</u>.

Special Test Section

Come
1 come down with
2 come into
3 come up against
4 come in for
5 come across

Get
1 get by
2 getting (me) down
3 get away with
4 get on with
5 get down

Give
1 gave away
2 gave up
3 gave away
4 gave out
5 gave in

Go
1 went on
2 go off
3 going on
4 goes up
5 gone through

Look
1 look after
2 look (it) up
3 looked for
4 looked (me) over
5 looking into

Pick
1 pick (you) up
2 pick out
3 pick on
4 pick up
5 picked up

Put
1 put off
2 put (me) up
3 put (me) down
4 put (me) through
5 put up with

Take
1 took (a year) off
2 takes after
3 take up
4 taking over
5 taken in